DEMYSTIFYING the FRENCH

How to Love Them, and Make Them Love You
(What you've heard about them is not entirely true...)

by

Janet Hulstrand

WINGED WORDS PUBLISHING

www.wingedwordseditorial.wordpress.com

Print ISBN 978-1-54395-351-0

eBook ISBN 978-1-54395-352-7

For any inquiries regarding this book, please email:

janet.hulstrand@gmail.com

For all those wonderful Frenchmen and women
who have given me the benefit of the doubt
time and time again, even when I forgot to say Bonjour.
Merci de votre compréhension!

TABLE OF CONTENTS

ACKNOWLEDGEMENTS

First a tip of the hat to the writers who helped me understand the French better myself, especially Julie Barlow and Jean-Benoît Nadeau, Polly Platt, Harriet Welty Rochefort, and Sally Adamson Taylor. I also want to thank those friends and fellow Americans who enthusiastically agreed to answer my questions on the flimsiest of information about what I planned to do with their answers when I first set out to write this book. For this and for many other acts of kindness, friendship, and professional support, I am deeply grateful to David Downie, Karen Fawcett, Ellen Hampton, Gary Lee Kraut, Adrian Leeds, Harriet Welty Rochefort, and Penelope Rowlands, not only for having shared their invaluable insights and perspective for this book, but for a multitude of other kind and supportive acts in past years. *Mille mercis!* Thanks also to Mary Winston Nicklin and *Bonjour Paris* for giving me the opportunity to interview so many interesting writers, and for permission to quote from some of those interviews in this book. Finally, for answering my questions from the French "side of the fence," I am grateful to Thierry Boussard who, with imagination and keen insight taught my boys and so many other boys to speak French, and to enjoy doing so (!)

Many thanks also to the BookBaby team, especially to Matthew Idler for his patience, encouragement, and expert guidance through the process. I also want to thank Susan Keselenko Coll, and Politics and Prose bookstore, for the opportunity to teach classes there. Teaching at P&P was truly one of the most satisfying parts of my life in Washington: it gave me the opportunity to begin to organize my thoughts about France and the French, as well as to share what I had learned with others—a most rewarding experience!

As she has done throughout my career, Anne Kostick provided excellent general editorial advice and guidance; and Ginnie Cooper's encouragement and support was key to the publication of this book. I am also grateful to Stephen Rueckert for his support and friendship over the past 40 years (and for a couple of the anecdotes included here). And to my sons Phineas and Sam Rueckert, just for being who they are, and for nodding approvingly—and instantly—when I told them I was going to write this book. ("You'd be good at that," they said.) You two are simply the best.

"Compare then, I say, as often as the occasion presents itself...
the process is both instructive and entertaining..."

- HENRY JAMES

INTRODUCTION

A friend of mine once told me that during the course of a conversation with a friend of hers, for some reason the friend (who is neither French nor American) said, "You know, it's funny about the French and the Americans. Both of them always think they're right about everything."

Not surprisingly, as an American, I was surprised by this remark. Though I love France and I have spent a great deal of my adult life there, I would never in a million years think of Americans being compared to the French in this way.

Though I love the French and admire many things about them, I think of them as "requiring special handling," whereas I think of Americans as being easygoing, freewheeling, and much more flexible in their approach to life. I don't think of us as holding to a "right" way of doing things—in fact, in my mind, that's one of the best things about us—whereas the French place a great deal of importance on being "*correct*."

But however you look at it, one sad fact of life is that Americans traveling in France often get "off on the wrong foot" with the French people they encounter almost instantly: this often leads them to believe that all those nasty things they've heard about the French are true—for example, that they are rude; arrogant; and that they hate Americans. (These unfortunate encounters also lead the French to believe that Americans are pretty rude too, though Americans tend to not even be aware of this.)

None of these things are true. In fact, I have tried to protect my French friends from the knowledge that many Americans feel this way, because I think it would hurt their feelings, and would also be simply incomprehensible to them.

In any case, it doesn't have to be this way! With just a little bit of specialized knowledge about what the French expect in terms of good manners, Americans (as well as other foreigners) can pretty easily get off on the right foot in France. And that can lead to one of the most pleasant experiences I can imagine. In fact, for me spending time in France has been so pleasurable that I've had a hard time talking myself into going anywhere else for many years now.

A few years ago I was given the opportunity to teach a class at Politics and Prose bookstore in Washington D.C., in which I shared some of the knowledge I had gained over the years about "getting along in France." In this class, which was called "Demystifying the French," and in a follow-up class, "Parlez-Vous Anglais? Survival French and French Travel Tips," I gave my students a few basic pointers about how to do a better job of dealing with the French, and I wrote a few blog posts to accompany the classes. This book began with those few posts, in which I offered a few simple "rules of the road" I've come up with, based on nearly 40 years of learning how to get along better in France.

The first part of the book is simple: five essential tips that I believe are necessary for even the briefest of encounters with the French, with brief explanations of the psychology, history, or reasoning behind the tips.

The second part of the book goes deeper and into much more detail about what makes the French "tick." In this part I've told stories about some of the things that have happened to me, or that I have observed, or heard about from others. I decided to ask some of my American friends in France as well, people who have lived here for a long time, about some of the kinds of situations that come up frequently, and that cause confusion, embarrassment, or just plain misunderstandings between French people and Americans, and to explore with them some of the fascinating aspects of this very interesting people.

Several of these friends reminded me, before answering my questions, that to make cultural generalizations is of limited value, and always introduces the risk of sliding into stereotyping. Before answering his questions, David Downie said, "Generalizations are dangerous. I try to avoid them. But like everyone else I wind up using them as a form of shorthand." Gary Lee Kraut struggled with some of my questions too, pointing out that "Life in France is more diverse than your questions imply." But he kindly agreed to try to play the game, because he's a nice guy and a good friend. "Inhabitants of France are less likely to get shot, less likely to have a household income over $100,000, less likely to be obese, less likely to worry about health insurance," he said. He added, "They are also more likely to smoke, more likely to study or learn some history, more likely to be an atheist or nonreligious, more likely to have vacation, more likely to be asked to comply with regulations, more likely to spend more time sharing a meal, etc." He concluded, "I suppose you can add these things up and get a difference."

Of course it's true, and valid, and important to remember that generalizations are of limited value, and that wherever you are in the world you are always dealing with individuals, and that individuals tend to stubbornly refuse to conform to stereotypes.

But I agree with Henry James, anyway, in feeling that the process is nonetheless both instructive and entertaining.

As I was writing, I realized that a glossary of common French words and phrases could be extremely useful to Americans traveling in France also. So the third section of the book is a glossary. I hope you find it helpful!

I've learned how to get along better in France by (often embarrassing) trial and error, along with some help from cultural guides who have gone before me. It is my hope that by sharing the wisdom I've gained along the way I can save you some of the embarrassment I've suffered, and help you get on the fast track to enjoying a wonderful culture and people—the French.

Janet Hulstrand

ESSOYES (L'AUBE) FRANCE

SEPTEMBER 2018

A note to the reader. Technically, in order to write French correctly, negative statements should use the "*ne....pas*" construction that anyone who has ever studied French has been taught. However, in real-life conversation in France you *hardly ever* hear the "*ne*" part of it. For that reason, I have decided to omit the "*ne*" most of the time, so that what you see in this book more closely resembles what you will hear. I hope this is okay with everyone.

And one caveat. The opinions expressed in this book are (obviously) mine. It is possible that some of them are wrong—and even more likely that some of them are oversimplified, and/or quite arguable. I have tried as much as possible to avoid making statements that are patently ridiculous, and I have tried not to say too much about things I don't know anything (or much) about. I hope I have achieved these goals at least. I have also tried to direct readers toward more reliable, more knowledgeable sources on the topics under discussion when I know how to do so.

Having said **all that**, I hope that my observations of a people and a culture I love and deeply respect will be helpful to those who would like to understand them better, and that better understanding will lead to more pleasant interactions with the French. (All too often they get a bum rap, they really do.) That was my main goal in writing this book, and if I've achieved that for even a handful of people, I will be happy. - JJH

PART ONE:
ESSENTIAL TIPS FOR EVEN VERY BRIEF ENCOUNTERS

Tip Nº 1.
Instead of smiling,
say Bonjour!

When I was first visiting, and then living for short periods of time in France, many years ago, I spent a lot of time walking out of the little shops in the small town outside of Paris where I was staying, wondering what I had done wrong.

I knew—well, I *sensed strongly*—that I had done *something* wrong, but I really couldn't imagine what it was. I always tried my best to smile nicely, to say please and thank you, and to use the very best French that I could.

But all of that wasn't enough, it seemed.

Then, many years later, a friend gave me the gift of Polly Platt's book, *French or Foe? Getting the Most Out of Visiting, Living and Working in France,* and *voilà!* All of a sudden I KNEW! And believe it or not, this is what I had been doing wrong:

Nine times out of ten, I had not been starting out by saying Bonjour.

Who could have imagined how important this small thing (to me) could be to the French?

Well, let me tell you: it's important, and it matters!! (And it's not a small thing to them.)

Tip #1 is THE MOST IMPORTANT thing anyone going to France can possibly know. Saying *bonjour* before you say ANYTHING ELSE will make more of a difference in how well you are treated there, and the quality of your social interactions in France than most Americans would believe possible, and it is so very easy to do!

It's even better to say "*Bonjour, Madame*" (or "*Bonjour, M'sieur*"). Or "*Bonjour, mesdames, messieurs*" (the plural). My friend Penelope Rowlands explains this by saying that these words are "an instant mark of respect, and people will respond accordingly."

You shouldn't forget to also say "*Merci*" and "*Au revoir*" as you are leaving, especially if you ever wish to return to the same shop, or see that person again.

It is really hard for Americans to understand how very important this simple act can be. But really, remembering to properly greet (and say goodbye to) the people that you encounter in your daily interactions in France is incredibly important.

This means EVERYONE. The person you ask for directions on the street. The *monsieur* or *madame* at the drive-through window in a "*MacDo's*" (McDonald's). Bus drivers. Even the security guard at the airport, of whom you are asking an urgent question in an attempt to avoid missing your plane. OBVIOUSLY the people who serve you in the *patisserie, boulangerie*, etc., etc., etc.

It's just part of treating someone like a human being, in France.

Americans tend to smile at strangers as a way of conveying the information that we are friendly, polite people who mean no harm.

But this smiling-at-a-stranger does no good at all in France, because smiling has an entirely different meaning there, as Polly Platt explained so well. In *French or Foe?* she quoted her French son-in-law expressing a typical French point of view on the matter: "When I am introduced to another man, if he smiles, then I think to myself one of three things: he is making fun of me, he is hypocritical, or he is very stupid. If it's a woman there's a fourth possibility—she wants to flirt."

Bonus Tip: *What do you say if you've already said "bonjour" and then you see the same person again later that day, or even five minutes later, as you cross paths once again in the street? You can say "rebonjour." Some older people might look a bit puzzled if it's the first time they've heard it, but it is becoming a common way among younger people to show that you are perfectly aware you have already acknowledged this person's humanity and wished them well for the day: and that you just want to do it again. It will usually draw a smile.*

One of the students in one of my Politics and Prose classes who has spent a great deal of time in France said that to a French person, forgetting to say *bonjour* is almost like a slap in the face. It's that bad!

People (including French people) do change over time, manners and habits evolve, and many people who carefully observe social customs say that the French are lightening up a little bit in this regard, and changing their ways. Consequently, some of the things Polly Platt wrote back in 1994 when *French or Foe?* was first published may be a bit outdated today.

Still. Don't count on your dazzling smile to charm the French the way it charms your fellow Americans. (Unless, of course, your purpose in smiling is flirting.)

If, on the other hand, you can manage to remember to begin each social interaction in France with a proper greeting ("Bonjour, Monsieur") and end the encounter with a proper farewell ("Au revoir, Madame"), you will find yourself feeling instantly and astonishingly more at ease in France, while also contributing to an improvement in the reputation of Americans in France. Not bad for a few simple little words!

Bonus Tip: *It helps to ensure that your "bonjour" will be heard if you adopt the same (beautiful) lilting tones the French use in saying it. If you mumble, or try to move past the "bonjour" too quickly, they simply may not hear you, and then it will be as if you haven't said it at all. Go ahead, you can do it! It may feel unnatural to **you**, but it's not hard to do, and it will make a difference. I promise!*

Here's the thing: despite knowing all this for at least 20 years now, I still make the mistake of forgetting to start with *Bonjour* fairly often. (I know! What is **wrong** with me?!) But I have found that when you forget, usually one of two things will happen: the French person may completely ignore your *faux pas* (but they probably won't be able to think less of you for it); or they may correct you.

The way they correct you is by pausing, giving you a hard, level stare, and then saying, "Bon-joooour," drawing out the second syllable nice and long. I would loosely translate this as, "I think you forgot something important, how about we back up?"

I have found that the best thing to do in this case is to instantly and sincerely apologize, and try to make up for it by saying,"Oui, bonjour, m'sieur, je suis desolée. J'ai oublié..."

When it happens with someone I know, they are more likely to give me a kind of "Really?!" look, and as soon as I see that look, I realize I've forgotten AGAIN! So I just apologize, sincerely and more or less profusely, using plenty of body language—hands in an "I surrender" pose, abject posture, etc.—to show I really mean it. "Je suis desolée, I forgot! You know, it's because I'm américaine..."

Then they smile, they understand, and they forgive...they do!

Tip № 2.
Ask "Do you speak English?"
before speaking English (!)

Another thing Americans do is to assume that everyone speaks English, and just start asking questions of the nearest person, in English.

I see this all the time, and it is just plain wrong, on so many levels.

First of all, in France you are supposed to start any social interaction with *Bonjour*. Remember? The all-important Tip #1?

Secondly, it would be great if you followed your *Bonjour* with an *Excusez-moi de vous déranger...*

But okay, maybe that's getting a bit too advanced, too quickly. We'll get to that. First let's just address the most egregious part of this problem.

How is it fair (or even semi-rational) to address a French person, in France, in English, before even asking them if they speak English?

Obviously, it's not.

So. Ideally, you should first ask them (preferably in French) if they speak English. It's not hard to say: *Parlez-vous anglais?* (Par-lay voo ahn-glay?).

Then they at least feel they have a *choice* in the matter. They also have time to prepare themselves to speak a foreign language.

You would want that for yourself, wouldn't you? If you were just minding your own business, in your own country, you wouldn't want someone to come up to you and just start speaking a foreign language, and assume that you understood them, would you? You'd think that was pretty presumptuous, and well, just plain rude, wouldn't you?

Okay, then. 'Nuf said. Practice saying *Parlez-vous anglais?* and see how much better things go the next time you're in France. (If you really can't bear to try the French, at least ask the question in English before launching into conversation.)

And if you really can't bear to try the French, maybe you can use that reluctance of yours to better understand what a kind (and difficult) thing French people are doing for you when they agree to speak English with you.

It's only fair. *N'est-ce pas?*

Tip № 3.
"Excuse me for
deranging you, but..."

In *French or Foe?* Polly Platt urged her readers to learn what she called the "ten magic words," words that she promised would open the doors of the French heart and soul, and turn potentially sour encounters into sweet ones.

Here are the first five words: *Excusez-moi de vous déranger...* (And no, it does not mean "Excuse me for deranging you." It means "I'm sorry to bother you.")

Starting an encounter with a stranger like this—for example, a person on the street who you want to ask for directions—lets them know two things.

1. You speak at least some French; and

2. You have good manners (that is, you are *bien élevé*). (*There will be more on this in Chapter 4.*)

But for now, with these two important facts established, you're off to a very good start.

Polly Platt said that, counter to their reputation of being aloof, condescending, and cold, if you add the next five words "*...monsieur, mais j'ai un problème,*" most French people will go quite far out of their way to try to help you solve it.

Penelope Rowlands mentioned these same words when I asked her about the most important things Americans should know when going to France. "Never approach a French person on the street, or indeed anywhere else, without first apologizing for the interruption," she said, and added, "The words *Excusez-moi de vous déranger* work magic. There's a perimeter around many French people, who tend to be reserved with people they don't know. When a stranger breaks into this personal space it feels to them like a violation." (She also said, "Never EVER EVER talk about money!" But we'll get to that in Chapter 8.)

As someone who grew up in the American Midwest, where many people are quite taciturn, when I first read this advice, my initial reaction was: *There is no way I can say that many words right off the bat.* (Followed by the thought: *And even if I could, surely they would know I had just been reading Polly Platt...*)

But. Then one day, in desperation, I decided to try it.

And you know what? Polly Platt was right. And so is Penelope.

Try it, and you'll see!

Tip № 4.
The importance of being pretty...(and don't worry, EVERYONE can be pretty!)

Why is Paris one of the most beautiful cities in the world?

Well, that is largely because people in France care about the way things look, and they pay close and careful attention to it—down to the smallest detail, pretty much all the time.

My favorite story about this is the time I went to a photocopy shop in Paris, to have copies made of a handout for class. The *monsieur* began (of course) by running a test copy. He carefully placed the original—just so!—on the plate glass, closed the cover, pushed the button and waited. But when the copy came out, "*Ooh la la,*" he said, shaking his head ruefully. A speck of lint—or something—on the glass had made a tiny mark on the copy. "Oh, monsieur, *c'est pas grave,*" I assured him. (Typically, as an American, I was in a hurry to get to class.) "*Mais non, madame, c'est pas jolie!*" ("It's not pretty!") he protested, as he reached for his glass cleaner, carefully cleaned the glass off, and tried again, this time producing a test copy that met his standard of excellence, and handing it to me for inspection, clearly pleased with the result. (Also, just as clearly, hoping for an appreciative remark from me, rewarding him for the care he had taken in the task. Which, of course, taking care to curb my impatience, I provided.)

On the upside, this careful attention to detail means that everywhere you look in France, things are arranged in such a way as to please the eye, from the grand architectural design of Paris to the artfully composed and colorful shop windows, to the way your food is presented, to the way people dress, with delightful visual detail an important part of the whole experience.

On the downside, you can't run down to the corner *patisserie* in sweatpants, hair awry, before you've made yourself presentable for the day, and expect to earn anyone's respect. Because presenting your unpresentable self in a public place is in itself considered disrespectful–to the people you are dealing with, to the values of the culture you are functioning in, and also to yourself.

No one (well, almost no one) is going to treat you rudely just because your physical presentation isn't what it should be in their eyes. That wouldn't be considered *correct* either, and being *correct* is important in France. (More on this in Chapter 4.) But some of the famous French coldness that Americans are talking about all the time may actually be a kind of instinctive recoiling from the shockingly (to them) casual way we present ourselves in public–and possibly dismay at our failure to do our part to make our little corner of the world–our part in the composition, as it were–a more beautiful place.

Looking good is important in France. It's not an accident that every French home I've ever been in has a lot of mirrors! This is not about having expensive clothing or the latest fashions. And it's not about having any particular classic kind of beauty or handsomeness either. It's about dressing in a way that is tasteful and visually interesting, and carrying yourself in a way that makes you look (and feel) your best.

So, while it's nice to be able to be accepted "for yourself" however you look, à l'américain, there's also something kind of nice about taking the time to look good. Especially in France, where people value the effort, and appreciate the result.

Tip № 5.
Shhh!!! (For goodness sake!)

This is one of the tips that is perhaps both hardest to understand, and—probably consequently—hardest for Americans to remember. But it is a very important one, both in terms of improving your own experience in France, and in terms of improving our national reputation.

French people tend to speak at a much lower decibel level, and in general make much less noise when in public, than we do. Because they do, it is first of all not necessary to speak as loudly in public places as Americans are used to doing. (Why? Because if everyone speaks more quietly, everyone else doesn't have to bellow in order to be heard. It's kind of amazingly wonderful!)

You will no doubt find, if you are ever so lucky as to spend a good deal of time in Paris that one day you will be sitting in a café somewhere, enjoying the soft murmur of nearby conversation, the quiet clinking of silverware and glasses, the ambient noise of the nearby street. Or you may be strolling along the Seine, enjoying the beauty of the view, the river barges passing by, the beautiful, luminous open sky. And gradually, for some reason you do not initially understand, you will feel your brow furrowing, and you will begin to feel irritated, you know not why.

And then suddenly you will know: it is a group of your countrymen (or women) that has burst your bubble of quiet contentment at being in this beautiful place: they are cackling, they are shouting, they are saying embarrassing things at the top of their lungs.

"Ay-yay-yay..." you will sigh.

So. Just know this. We all tend to talk more loudly than we need to. We don't mean anything bad by it, we can't help it, it's just a bad habit. And it's not a problem at home.

But it is when we are traveling in France. It's actually kind of obnoxious.

Unfortunately, it's all too easy to do when we find ourselves in a place that has made us so happy, so excited! And we are among friends, whether new ones or old!

But. Try to remember to keep the volume down, okay?

The payoff? You may see—and hear—things you wouldn't have seen or heard, if you hadn't taken the trouble to follow this tip.

So try it! *Pourquoi pas?*

PART TWO:
UNDERSTANDING THE
FRENCH MENTALITY

1

DO THEY REALLY NOT UNDERSTAND ME? (OR ARE THEY JUST BEING MEAN?)

Let's begin by saying that there is *nothing easy* about French pronunciation.

Unlike at least some other Romance languages—Italian and Spanish, for example—French pronunciation is not uncomplicated and perfectly reliable. You can't just learn the five vowel sounds and count on them to remain the same, predictably, reliably, in fact *almost always*.

French is full of weird diphthongs, vowel combinations that force a person to screw his or her mouth into shapes that most Anglophones find, quite frankly, just ridiculous.

So the first thing is, you have to get over that.

And you should also get over the sneaking suspicion that when French people give you that quizzical look—you know the one I mean—that pained expression that seems to say, "I have no idea what you're talking about"—most of the time it is probably not because *they* are being difficult. It is because their *language* is a difficult one, and they really *are* trying to figure out what you're trying to say.

The French language really is just **that difficult.** Those vowels and vowel combinations mentioned above can be devilishly hard to distinguish from each other, and especially to *pronounce*.

Here's an example. Recently a friend of mine was planning a trip to France and was preparing herself by reviewing what she knew about the French language. "You're the one who taught me about *boeuf*," she said. "I did??" I said, doubtfully. "What did I teach you about *boeuf*?" I was trying to imagine why I would have been teaching her about the French word for beef. "Yes! You taught me that that's what they say all the time," she said, repeating *boeuf*, but this time adding a shrug of her shoulders that she no doubt remembered went along with *boeuf*. "Oh, you mean *bfff*!" I said. Now it made sense.

And she gave me that look Anglophones often have when trying to master the subtleties of French pronunciation, as I smiled and said, "Well *bfff*, that's not **at all** the same as *boeuf*." (For an explanation of the very rich meaning of *bfff*, see the Glossary.)

The thing is, French is difficult not only to pronounce (physically), especially for Anglophones. It is also difficult to know how to render something you have heard in French in writing, or to decode something you have heard spoken. (This is as true for French people as for anyone else.) There are usually a host of possibilities. (I am not going to try to explain this any further here, in this book.

Maybe in another one devoted simply to speaking French; for now you'll have to just trust that what I am saying here is true.)

So, if nothing else, you can know from the get-go that learning French is going to be *very good* for your brain. Because there's a lot of mental exercise involved in learning to speak French.

The first time I arrived in Paris, as one of my first excited acts, I went into a bookstore and asked for a copy of a volume of poems by my favorite French-language poet, Guillaume Apollinaire. Apollinaire wasn't that hard to say, but the title of the collection I was looking for, *Alcools*, was then, and remains for me now, almost impossible to say well enough that a French person can understand what I'm saying. (The difficulty is in those two "o's" next to each other: and no. It is *not* pronounced the way we pronounce two o's together.) And so the salesperson gave me that quizzical look—the furrowed brow, the slight frown, the cocked head. And, crestfallen, I had to write it down for him. "Ah! *Alcools! par Apollinaire!*" he said, face brightening, as he headed toward the right shelf.

Well, yes, isn't that what I had said? Apparently not, or in any case, **not well enough.**

I hate to admit it, but even though my accent is *not that bad*, I guess it's not that good either. Because this kind of thing *still* happens to me, after nearly forty years of spending as much time in France as I can, and speaking the language as well as I can. And having poured tons of energy into the endeavor.

One of the hardest things about learning a language really well is, well, just how hard it is. Another thing that is hard is accepting the fact that you are probably never going to speak it perfectly no matter how hard you try, not if you started as an adult. So, when you find yourself realizing a couple of minutes after the fact (for example) that you have just told someone who was showing you the paintings by local artists that they are collecting, that you have said (approvingly), "Oh yes, it's important to *supprimer les artistes*" (which means to suppress, cancel, or delete them), instead of to *soutenir* (support) them, just be glad that they probably know you didn't mean what you said at all. Or if you find yourself wondering whether you've just said before (*avant*) or after (*après*)—opposites really shouldn't start with the same letter should they?!—you should know that you are not alone.

So. The main point of this chapter is to let you know that a) They aren't kidding, the French. If you don't pronounce certain words with exactly the right subtle nuance(s), there are about a million things other than what you're trying to say that your listener may be having to sift through to figure out what you mean. And b) You are certainly not alone.

Also: if you would like to know how to say some of the trickiest words in the French language, or if you ever plan to go to any of these three places in France, you should go to the Glossary, and look up Reims. And Caen. And Cannes. Then listen to them over and over, until you can first hear how they are pronounced—there are lots of ways to listen to the correct pronunciation on the Internet—and then hopefully, one day, you will be able to pronounce them correctly.

In the meantime, relax, and just do the best you can. You'll get better, in time.

You might want to keep a pencil in your pocket, and a piece of paper always handy, until then.

2

THE INCOMPREHENSIBLE
APPEAL OF THE NEGATIVE

By the time you've gotten the basics under control, you may have developed something of a curiosity about French people. And if you're anything like me, that curiosity, and that fascination with their wonderfully complex psychology, will keep you pleasantly occupied with trying to understand them, and to make your interactions with them—despite their famous reputation for pessimism, negativity, and just plain orneriness—as positive as they can possibly be, for the next half-century or so.

One of the things that especially Americans tend to notice about the French right away is that they seem to approach almost every situation in a negative manner. "C'est impossible!" or "C'est pas possible!" they cry. Or—when they're a bit more willing to admit there might be a chance, a small, a very, very **small** chance of success—they might say, often with a deep sigh, "C'est pas évident."

Through the years I have heard many anecdotes, and expressions of amazement by Americans, that things that are so very clearly not only not impossible, but are very very **very** possible, and in fact sometimes **downright easy!!!!** are dismissed out of hand as being *impossible* by the French.

Recently a friend who was coming to visit me in the small French village where I now live recounted such an incident. In asking me what I found so charming about the French, he said, "But they seem to always start from the position that everything is impossible." When I smiled and agreed with him, he told me how just then, as he and his friends were trying to find their way to my house, they had stopped and asked someone for directions. He then mimicked a dramatic demonstration of the impossibility of the situation this Frenchman believed my friends were in—all exaggerated Gallic shrugs, incredulous puffs of breath, and exasperated shakes of the head. My American friend concluded his story by saying, "And then after all that, he just pointed at the next road, and said, 'Turn right up there.'"

"The French are the only people I know of who have a negative way of saying yes," says another friend, and although that description is not entirely accurate, it's true that when you ask someone a question in French that is posed in a negative way—for example, "You don't happen to have a pen, do you?"—the way to answer "yes" is not *oui*, but *si*. It's just one of those funny little details about the French language that allows you to feel very satisfied with yourself when you manage to get the hang of it, and remember to answer *si* in most, if not all, situations where it is called for.

Bonus Tip: *The French do NOT adhere to the belief that "the customer is always right." They just don't. Americans in particular waste a lot of time and energy being annoyed about this. I believe the time is better spent finding a way to charm the French into being nice to you. It is very satisfying when you can* *manage to do this, especially if you can bring someone who you are dealing with from a position of surliness or disdain to one of pleasant helpfulness. This is quite an accomplishment: if you manage to do it, good for you!*

The most important thing to know about this negativity of the French is discussed in a most helpful way in Julie Barlow and Jean-Benoît Nadeau's book *The Bonjour Effect: The Secret Codes of French Conversation Revealed*. In the chapter tellingly titled, "Finding the Yes in Non," they say that the French say no "...everywhere, all the time...They say no when they mean yes. And they say no when they want you to think they might eventually say yes. The trick is in understanding the many things 'no' can actually mean."

Their book is very worth reading, so I won't try to capture any more of what they say about that here. But I will say that shortly after reading it, I realized what I had done wrong in a certain situation. It had to do with the very new (in France) concept of taking uneaten food away with you when you leave a restaurant. The "doggy bag" concept was until recently never practiced in France, and it was in fact considered bad manners to ask to bring food home. In France you are supposed to enjoy your meal, appreciate it thoroughly, and finish it, in a very leisurely way. You are not supposed to leave half of it on the plate and then ask to take some home with you.

However, in keeping with a growing concern in France to minimize food waste, in 2016 it actually became law that restaurant owners have to comply when they are asked to wrap something up for a customer and send it home with them.

So, when I had a meal out with a bunch of friends and I really could not finish my (very tasty) meal, I thought I would try to get over my decades-old training in not asking to take it home, and simultaneously test the new law. When the waiter, who was giving me plenty of time to enjoy and finish my meal finally came and motioned to my still-pretty-full plate, I asked him if I could take it home with me. "*Je peux pas, Madame. J'ai pas les moyens.*" ("I can't, ma'am. I don't have any way to do that") he said, with a dismissive toss of his head, adding one of those no-can-do Gallic shruggings of the shoulders for good measure.

What did I do? I instantly retreated into my default, do-not-make-a-fuss Midwestern mentality, and meekly accepted the verdict, though I was truly annoyed. I *knew* it was the law, and I *knew* it was perfectly possible for him to find a way to send the food home with me—the French are nothing if not creative and resourceful. And I had really been looking forward to having a very fine lunch of my leftovers the next day.

It was only the next day—around lunchtime—that the light bulb went on in my head, and I remembered Barlow and Nadeau. "When the French vehemently disagree with something, it doesn't mean the conversation is over," they say. "It's more like a conversation starter, a bargaining position, or an invitation to make a counter-offer. The mistake is to consider *non* a stone wall, when it actually operates like a trampoline."

How right they are!

I realized in retrospect that I had accepted the waiter's *non* as a stone wall when what I should have done is recognized it as the opening line in a negotiation, and said something like, "*Mais, monsieur, pourquoi?*" making room for a conversation to begin, about how the food really was good, but I really couldn't have another bite, not right now...and then there is that new law, and....and so on. If I had done that, I probably would have been able to walk away from the table with my food, and still have left the waiter in a more or less good mood. Because he would have enjoyed the back and forth of the conversation. (One thing we might have discussed is whether or not this restaurant was subject to that law. The law is not universally applicable: it depends on certain specific factors, such as size of the restaurant, and so on: French rules are nothing if not complicated.)

So that piece of wisdom from Barlow and Nadeau is something I will definitely try to remember from now on. And in fact, in other similar situations I have been more successful in turning no into yes.

For example, there was the time I needed to find a place to allow the students in my study abroad class in Paris to make their final oral presentations to each other. We had planned to do this in the park, but when the day came, the weather was not conducive to being outside. So I went to the administrative assistant of the dorm we were staying in, and presented my dilemma, stating in advance that I hoped he could give me *conseil* (advice). (I have found it is often much more effective to ask for *conseil* than to ask for a favor. Most people *like* to give advice!)

I explained the situation, and asked if we might be able to use one of the empty rooms upstairs for an hour. The first thing he said was standard, by the book, and very officious. "Oh, for that you'll have to get permission from the central office," he said. "We can't make any arrangements like that from here."

Hmm. I did not argue with him, just shook my head doubtfully, kind of sadly, really; and noted how that sounded pretty *compliqué* (complicated), and how since my students would be gathering in just ten minutes, that solution was probably not going to work very well for me.

Now I had him on my side. (Because, as Polly Platt claimed— correctly—the French actually love creative problem solving, and they like helping people. They also certainly understand the challenge of dealing with something that is *compliqué*. There will be more about this in Chapter 3.)

"Well," he suggested. "You could perhaps go over to the big commons building, and find a *hall* somewhere off to the side, something that is not a *room*, and do it there?" He looked at me hopefully, to see what I thought of this idea.

"Mmm," I said, "Yes, I guess we could try to do that." But I still looked a bit doubtful, and while I was thinking about what I should say next, he proposed something even better. "Or, you know, you could meet in the hallway right outside my office here. That wouldn't bother me."

"Really?" I said. He smiled (that charming French smile!) and I gushed, "Oh, m'sieur, *c'est gentil!* (you're so kind). *Merci beaucoup!*"

And so my students did their presentation in the hall outside the residence hall office. "We can't go into one of those empty rooms upstairs?" one of them asked. "There's no one in there..." (A typically American, typically practical approach to the situation...)

"Non!" I said, now taking the side of my generous, gallant Frenchman. "*C'est pas autorisé.*"

What many Americans would do in such a situation, of course, is to argue with the authority in question. Americans can get very stuck on practicalities. Why *couldn't* we use the upstairs room that no one was going to be using for the one hour we needed it? Who would know? Who would care?

But that wasn't the point. The main reason we couldn't do that is because we were in France. And in France, rules count (kind of).

But the French *do* love finding ways to get around them. (See *Système* D in the Glossary for more on this.)

They also can be extraordinarily adept at creative problem solving, and willing to help, especially if you ask in just the right way. They just have to go through that whole "it's impossible" thing first.

"The French themselves are troubled and baffled by their incurable gloominess, pessimism, and melancholy. The three are not exactly the same, of course, but they're related...Where does this bleakness originate? I'm sure it has countless origins. Usually it's attributed to the educational system, which pits students against each other from an early age. The society here is very competitive and fairly heartless. If you're struggling you'll be helped to fail, someone will push you under as they clamber up and over you. For instance if you fail your 'bac' exam—needed for the French high school/junior college degree— you are pretty much lost. Kids go to school with prospective failure dangling over them, a Damocles sword that makes them anxious and gloomy. There is also a sense of the weight of the past—each French person is just part of a collective reality that's thousands of years old and will roll on indifferently with or without them. (But many other Europeans face the same reality, yet aren't as gloomy as the French, so this explanation doesn't quite convince me). Melancholy can be delicious, and the French as a general rule appear to glory in it, like lovelorn teenagers wallowing in sadness. It strikes outsiders as juvenile or adolescent, and perhaps it is, but it's one of the more endearing qualities of this nation. In other countries with a Gallic heritage the people don't seem obsessed with what I've called 'joie de tristesse,' or the thrill and joy of unhappiness. This phenomenon actually kind of short-circuits itself, because if melancholy makes people happy then maybe we simply need to redefine melancholy. One thing is sure: French notions of happiness, fulfillment, and joy do not make an identical match with those of Americans. But isn't that one of the things that makes France so fascinating?"

- DAVID DOWNIE

3

A PASSION FOR COMPLICATION

One of the tips I give my students is that they should, whenever possible, give the merchant exact change when buying something in France. "I do not know *why*, but I do know *that* French people really, really, **really** want you to give them exact change if you possibly can. They just do," I say.

This can lead to a confusing situation for Anglophones, because the word for "change" in French is *monnaie*. So if a French person looks at the money you have given them and says "*Vous n'avez pas de monnaie?*" you might understandably be confused. After all, haven't you just given them *monnaie*?

But, no, you see, you have not. You have given them *argent*, which means, literally, "silver," and is the word used for money. Or you have given them *espèce*, which means "cash"; but you have not given them exact change.

As I said, I really know don't why this obsession with getting exact change exists, where it comes from, or why it is so fervent.

But I do know *that* it exists, and that providing it is one way of getting on the right side of the French.

I had wondered about this idly for years, and then one day one of my students in my summer class in Paris asked my friend Ellen Hampton about this. Ellen is a writer who was visiting my class that day, and she was talking about her book *Playground for Misunderstanding*, which is a murder mystery that also deals a lot with Franco/American cultural differences. "Why do they always want exact change?" this student asked Ellen. Ellen, who is American, but who has lived in France for most of her adult life, nearly 30 years, didn't hesitate for a moment. "Oh!" she said, cheerfully. "That's because the French have a passion for complication."

Wow. What a moment of incandescent clarity! "That explains the matter of exact change and SO MUCH MORE!" I said, and added, "Thank you, Ellen!"

Bonus Tip: *French people will often comment on the complicated nature of the French language when they see you struggling with it. They are not only being very kind by trying to make you feel better about the trouble you are having: I believe they are also demonstrating in one more way that French "passion for complication." To the French, something that is complicated is interesting; and it is worthy of respect, not impatience or disdain. (There's more on this in Chapter 7.)*

Interestingly, while I was working on this book, one of the points made in a Facebook post that shared "interesting facts about France" was that there is actually a law that says French merchants are not required to give change to customers: it is up to the customers to have exact change. And while I have not been able to confirm that this is indeed a law, it was interesting to me that it was stated as one, and believed as such, by the person who posted it. And knowing how very regulated France is, I'm inclined to believe it myself until proven otherwise.

Another interesting development that occurred while I was writing this book is that the French Prime Minister, Edouard Philippe, announced a change in the way the French administration will be dealing henceforth with its citizens (at least during this *quinquinnat*, the five-year presidential term in France), in cases where certain administrative rules have not been followed. He referred to it as *le droit de l'erreur* (or, "the right to make a mistake"). I heard him give this speech on television, and I noticed he was saying, among other things, that the French government has been known for an excess of "complexities." The government spokesman who followed him to describe how the plan would unfold even used the word *manie* (which means "craziness," or maybe we would say in this case, "obsessiveness") to describe the French approach to governmental administration. What I have understood (so far) from reading about *le droit de l'erreur* is that basically the French government will be making an attempt to approach its citizens less with an attitude of "guilty until proven innocent" and more with an attitude that "anyone can make a mistake: ONCE!" Given the infamous complexities (indeed) of the French government, this seems only fair and right. Of course we shall see what follows!

Sometimes the complications of the French way of life seem to be inexplicable and completely needless wastes of time, until you give them a little more thought. For example, in order to renew my visa, one of the things I needed to complete the process was a certain amount in *timbres fiscaux* (official government stamps you must buy in order to make some official documents official). I was told that I could buy some of these stamps at the *tabac* next to the *Office de Tourisme*, about six blocks away from the *préfecture*. As I rushed to get there (and back) before the *préfecture* would close for lunch, so I could get my visa, I was shaking my head over the fact that you couldn't simply purchase these stamps in the same place you had to turn them in, that is, the *préfecture*. How impractical!

How silly! I was thinking. Until I realized that this was perhaps one more little way that the French government has devised to provide *tabacs* with business. (The French government does a lot of this putting-their-hand-on-the-scale kind of thing, to benefit a variety of small businesses.) No doubt the nice lady in the *tabac* who sold me the stamps gets a small commission every time she provides this service, I realized as I waited for her to count out the amount of stamps I needed. Was it so bad for me to have to walk six blocks to get them? No, it really wasn't. (Though it must be said: I know that I am lucky, in that walking does not present a problem for me; and that this is not so for everyone.)

Other times, there is no discernible reason for the scurrying around you have to do. Another step in getting my visa finalized was that I had to provide an official translation of my birth certificate, translated by an officially recognized translator. I was told that I could get a list of approved translators from the *tribunal* (which I managed to figure out was the *palais de justice*, in other words, the courthouse), about 10 blocks away. Since there was no financial transaction in this instance, and all I had to do at the *tribunal* was ask for a photocopied list of officially approved translators in my *département*, it was a little hard to understand why I had to go to the courthouse to get it. Why couldn't they just keep copies of the list at the *préfecture*? Or make the list available on the Internet? (Here is where Ellen's answer to the question comes in handy...)

I believe Ellen is right, by the way, in saying that it is a "passion" for complication. It is certainly not just resigned tolerance of it, though there is also that (*c'est la vie*). I believe this is an important point. Whereas Americans, an extremely practical people, tend to view complications as annoyances to be ignored, defied, destroyed, or otherwise defeated, I think it can be said that for most French people complication is more likely to be seen as a challenge to overcome: an opportunity to *se débrouiller*. (You will find an explanation of this very French concept in the Glossary).

In any case, I've spent enough time in France to know when it makes sense to ask questions, and when you should just do exactly what you have been told to do, if you want things to proceed smoothly. So I went to the courthouse and got the piece of paper I needed. And I contacted one of the officially approved translators. And I got my visa. YAY!!!!

> "In Paris there is an expectation that no matter how difficult the situation may become, you should be able to handle it. I would say there's a reverse expectation in the States sometimes: that it has to be made simple for you to get it. I like that life in Paris is challenging, and at the same time, I tear out my hair: Why can't they make it simple! Some of the conflict arises from the French affection for Cartesian thought. Going directly from point A to point B is not interesting, so let's take a tour by X, Y, and Z along the way. Traffic engineers do this to exasperating effect."
>
> - ELLEN HAMPTON

4

The Importance of Stability, Order, and Being Correct

Stability, order, and being correct are not exactly the same things, of course, but I think they are closely related enough to fit together in one chapter.

Jean-Baptiste Alphonse Karr is the Frenchman credited with creating the phrase "*plus ca change, plus c'est la même chose*" ("The more things change, the more they stay the same...") in 1849, which happened to be a time of great change in French history. But then again, maybe it wasn't? Or maybe it always is?

"Because the French are so socially progressive and liberal about relationships, they often are mistaken for liberals," says Ellen Hampton. "Yet French society is deeply, deeply conservative. Change is seen as just about the worst thing that can happen. The good side of that: Paris retains its historic charm. The bad side: work laws are designed for 19th century economics. Why the French do what they do almost always has historic roots, and newcomers are often unaware of them."

When I interviewed Craig Carlson, the American owner of the Breakfast in America chain of diners in Paris, for *Bonjour Paris*, he said almost exactly the same thing in answer to my question about what was so controversial about French president Emmanuel Macron's proposed changes in the *code du travail* (labor code). "The French will resist any change, no matter how small," he said.

As Ellen points out, there is a good side to the depth of the conservative instinct in French people: history is honored, tradition is held onto, change is made only very slowly, and with a great deal of thought and deliberation given to it first. When I returned to my little village in Champagne after 14 years away, I was afraid that I would find it greatly changed. But guess what? Although some changes had happened in the intervening years, technological advances had been kept apace with, and so on, everything *looked* pretty much the same. Walls and buildings centuries old had not changed at all, on the outside at least. There is not that build it, tear it down, start over, repeat cycle of mindless "progress" that has turned so much of the United States into an ugly wasteland less than 200 years after it was stolen from its rightful owners in pristine condition.

So what does it mean, this being "*correct*"?

Frequently the explanation given for why you can't do something in France is *on n'a pas le droit* ("one doesn't have the right"). You often hear French children shouting—or whispering—these words to each other. It's kind of the opposite of all those wild little American children at play, insisting they can do things they probably *aren't* allowed to do, by boasting, "It's a free country!"

When I asked my friend Adrian Leeds what she finds the most difficult about living in France, she did not hesitate for a second.

"What is most difficult for me is that French law—the Napoleonic code—is based on what is allowed, rather than what is forbidden, as it is with English law," she said. "This means that following the rules, even when they are ridiculous, takes precedence over logic. In other words," she explained, "to the American or British way of thinking, if something isn't forbidden, you can do it. But to the French, if something isn't specifically allowed, you probably can't do it. This makes people ridiculously cautious and unwilling to take chances."

One of the things that makes the French feel comfortable, secure, and stable is when they, and those around them, are behaving in a way that is seen (by the French) as being "*correct*." This alone indicates a major difference between the French view of life and the American one: being "correct" is something Americans don't spend very much time worrying about, and if they were very concerned about this, they'd have a problem on their hands, since what is "correct" behavior is nowhere nearly as clearly defined in the United States as it is in France.

French children are taught a myriad of small but important ways to act and interact on a daily basis, from the time they are very small children. Some of the first things they learn I have already covered in my essential tips. (Saying "*Bonjour, Madame*," (Tip #1), and keeping their voices moderated (Tip #5) are probably the two most important ones.)

The importance of being "correct" is probably one of the main reasons for the significantly different way that Americans raise their children, and French people do. In general, Americans find the French way of teaching children to behave almost shockingly harsh. And the French tend to find the American way of raising their children almost shockingly careless. "*Ils font n'importe quoi!*" they often say, about Americans ("They do just any old thing!"), and they say this not just in reference to the way we raise our children, but to the way we characteristically deal with just about anything at all.

It's a bit ironic, at least to me, that the people who made up the phrase *laissez faire* are so little prone to adopting a *laissez faire* attitude in their daily lives, but whatever. (You see how I said "whatever" just now? That is a *very* American attitude. Americans are much more prone to saying "whatever" than the French are.)

The French actually do believe in the importance of individual freedom, in many important ways. "Live and let live," a phrase that made its way into the lyrics of one of the Cole Porter songs in the musical *Can-Can*—which is about life in Gay Paree, in the dance halls of Montmartre—really is something the French firmly and deeply believe in. Their famous and very strong belief in the difference between public and private life, and the importance of protecting the latter from the scrutiny or judgment of others, is real.

Then again, when someone, whether an adult or a child, is behaving in public in a way that is not considered *correct* (by the French), look out! You (or the child) may very well be heading for some very frank criticism, some very public humiliation.

In his wonderful book, *Paris, Paris: Journey into the City of Light*, David Downie describes spending a full day in the Luxembourg Gardens, and says "a day spent loitering there teaches you more about Paris and its inhabitants than many a scholarly tome." One of the things he observes that day is a young boy who is at the famous boat pond with his grandmother, being soundly scolded by a park *gardien* when he has started to do what little boys WILL DO with sticks when they have them. (That is, use them as swords, in this case, a "sword" that was being used to scare the ducks.) Downie reports, "As the grandmother and her chastened grandson slunk off, I remarked to a neighbor in an upright chair that the *gardien* was perhaps too strict. '*Monsieur*,' my neighbor remonstrated, 'The rules must be enforced.'" What happened next, Downie tells us, is that "A chorus of Gallic voices agreed, 'Rules, rules, rules!'" Downie, who was, of course, also once a boy, an *American* boy, slunk off shortly afterward too, presumably also chastened, or at least not enjoying the company of his neighbors anymore.

When my boys were young and we were spending every summer in Paris, this cultural difference created some awkward situations. One summer, when my younger son was only two—two!—we took my students on a guided tour of Monet's home and gardens in Giverny. The tour began in Paris, and we went to Giverny on a tour bus. Shortly before we approached the village of Giverny, Sammy saw a herd of cows in a field, which brought him great delight. The problem came when we had passed the field and there were no more cows to be seen. "WAN' SEE COWS!" he cried out in his bois-terous little toddler voice, and he kept repeating the phrase over and over, the rest of the way to Giverny (which fortunately wasn't very far!). I tried everything imaginable to contain his enthusiasm, including holding my hand over his mouth, but it was just fated that everyone on that bus had to hear for the rest of the way, how much Sammy wanted to see cows.

It didn't seem to bother my American students all that much, in fact in general I think they were bemused. But as I got off the bus, with Sammy in my arms, I heard the tour guide, a rather stern, schoolmarmish Frenchwoman probably in her 50s, mutter, "*Mal élevé.*"

Mal élevé means "bad mannered," "ill-bred," or (literally) "badly raised," and it is quite an insult. I did not bother to respond to this insult on the spot: I was much more interested in attending to my child and to my students. But the insult burned, and to this day I really wish I had said to her, "You are wrong, *Madame*. My child is not *mal élevé*. He is not *élevé* at all. He is TWO! He is not finished yet."

And every once in a while I wish (ludicrously) that she could see what a fine young man he has turned into. He is *très bien élevé* indeed.

While like many Americans I do not really approve of the harsh tone French people often take in correcting even very young children, I have to admit that I have admired, even marveled, at the way even very small French children sit still for long periods of time in restaurants, behaving in an impeccable way that is—for the parents of typically active American youngsters—frankly kind of unfathomable. My own preference became to try to avoid restaurants until our kids were old enough to be able to sit still and actually enjoy being in them. Still, when we were in France every summer we ate out quite a lot, and I always wondered how French parents managed to teach their kids to sit so still, to be so quiet, so well-behaved at the table.

Then one day I saw something that I thought provided a little bit of an inkling into the way at least some French parents—and in this case probably a grandparent—did that. It was toward the end of a very hot summer day and I was in the Luxembourg Gardens. Ahead of me on the path was a girl who looked to be about six or seven. She was flanked by what seemed to be her mother and probably her grandfather (or else a very old father). And the girl was whining. She definitely was whining, as children will do, especially toward the end of a long, hot day, when they are tired. Suddenly, without warning, the grandfather raised his hand and smacked her—hard! Right across the face.

She stopped whining instantly. And I thought, "Hmm. *That's* how they do it." And I knew I wasn't going to do it that way. My feeling was that it might take longer to get your kids to be well-behaved if you didn't resort to slapping them. But in the end they still turn out fine.

However, I don't want to leave the impression that this obsession—or at least *strong emphasis*—on being "*correct*" is always negative. And now we're getting back to the subject of the importance of order, stability—and predictability.

The French are more or less right when they say that Americans *font n'importe quoi*. And this has its advantages. When everyone approaches life in more or less the way that feels the most comfortable to them, there's a wonderful freedom in that. But that freedom also leads to a kind of lack of social order, even chaos, and a lack of the kind of comfortable predictability that exists in France in a way that it certainly does not in the United States.

This was brought home to me once when we had a French high-school student staying with us for a couple of weeks as part of a school exchange program. It was a Sunday morning and I was making a pot roast for our lunch. But shortly before what would be considered lunchtime in France—which is quite specifically prescribed, and not very flexible—a neighbor called me and asked if I could help her daughter who was struggling to write an essay for a college application. The application was due the next day, and she was stuck.

I said, "Sure, come on over." So the daughter and her mother came over, and we talked about her essay for about an hour. Meanwhile, the pot roast was stewing.

Anyway. In the middle of our meeting, our French guest hesitantly, and politely interrupted us, wanting to know if we would be eating. "Yes, sure we will," I said in a way I hoped was reassuring, and smiling at him. But it was probably nearing 1:00 by then, and it probably seemed to him that we would be talking forever. And so, he still looked rather anxious.

Poor fellow! I assured him that it wouldn't be too much longer, and indicated the pot roast simmering on the stove. Now reassured, he looked relieved and retired to his room.

But I realized that to him this American free-wheelingness, especially about meals and mealtime, was probably pretty hard to understand. One of the most predictable things about life in France is that between noon and 2 p.m. almost everyone in France is going to be eating a meal. Not just "grabbing a bite." Not eating at their desks, or eating while strolling in the park, or riding the subway. Most French people, still to this day, whether in Paris or in small French villages, take a couple of hours out of the day, beginning around noon, to sit down and share a decent meal with someone: family, or coworkers, or whomever. They just do. And to not do so can be deeply unsettling. One of my favorite details from Diane Johnson's wonderful novel Le Divorce is a scene in which some French children have been involved in a rather dramatic situation that has kept them from having their noontime meal. Without revealing too much, I can say that the first thing they say when they are released from the situation is, "We haven't had our lunch!" And they are quickly hurried away, by the nearest Frenchwoman, to the nearest place where this problem can be corrected.

It has occurred to me that being an American living in France may perhaps—at least sometimes and in some ways—be preferable to being a French person living in France. After all, as an American living in France I am able to enjoy the orderliness and predictability of the French schedule, and all that implies—including knowing when I am likely to be interrupted by others, and when I am not, because everyone is eating (!). But I myself am not in any way enslaved to that schedule. I can still eat whenever I want to, and feel free to do other things whenever I want, in my insouciant, n'importe quoi American way. It's kind of an ideal situation, the best of both worlds.

I often tell my students that the French are wonderful people, and that they have many good qualities. But I always add, because it's true, "Flexibility is not one of them." Because in order to maintain the conditions which to the French represent stability, order, and a rather narrow code of polite behavior, a certain amount of inflexibility is required. And I think it is fair to say that generally speaking, Americans tend to be more flexible than the French. But I also have to add that I have seen French men and women respond in a most creative and flexible manner many times over the years, especially in situations that are important and that call for quick action.

It's the unimportant (to us!) little details of life they tend to get hung up on.

"The essential difference between French law and English or American law, is that English law is based on what is forbidden. The Napoleonic Code is based on what's allowed. This fundamental difference in our cultures is the basis of everything we Americans are confused by when we first encounter life in France. When we know what is forbidden, then we can openly imagine all that is possible, which encourages creative thinking and open-mindedness. When we only know what rules we must follow, and we are punished for thinking outside the box, or doing anything outside of those rules, it stifles our creativity and closes our minds to what is possible. The French see life this way, while we see life in exactly the opposite way. If there was one thing I could change, it would be this: it's the one thing that holds the French back from ruling the world."

- ADRIAN LEEDS

5

THE IMPORTANCE OF
TAKING YOUR TIME

This is probably one of the most fundamental differences between French and American life, and one of the most beautiful things about life in France. It is one of the things my New Yorker students notice first upon their arrival in Paris: that the pace of life is so much less hurried. (It's funny to compare their reaction to Paris and Parisians to what you always hear about Paris and Parisians in the French countryside: that "the pace of life in Paris is so hurried!" It's a question of perspective...)

But whether you are looking at life in Paris or in the French countryside, the French do not believe in rushing. They believe in taking one's time: to do things right (*correct*, or *comme il faut*); to do things well; to enjoy oneself; and especially to enjoy one's meals. This is what underlies the continuing French tradition of taking a nice long break at lunch to have a real, several-course meal. Even in Paris, to this day many businesses close for a couple of hours at lunch so that people can do this. In small towns and villages it is even more true, and the shops stay closed for a longer time. In my village pretty much everything is closed from 12:30-3:00, and in the case of the bakeries, until 4:30 or 5:00 p.m. (Think about how early the bakers have to get up to have fresh bread ready for everyone by 7 am! And then they stay open until 7:30 pm so everyone can get fresh bread again, for dinner. So they need a nice, long break in the afternoons.)

This is such an important aspect of life in France that there is even a verb to describe it: flâner. Sometimes this word is translated as "to stroll," and that's not a bad translation, but it is far too narrow. Harriet Welty Rochefort has a chapter in her book *Joie de Vivre: Secrets of Wining, Dining, and Romancing Like the French* called "Hanging Out Without Feeling Guilty." I think "hanging out without feeling guilty" is a perfect description of what it means to flâner: and a flâneur or flâneuse is a person who enjoys doing this.

Sometimes flâner is translated as "loitering," or "loafing," which tells you something about the different approach to life in Anglo-Saxon vs. Latin cultures. Hanging out without feeling guilty is certainly not loitering, and as Harriet stresses, it is not being lazy. It is enjoying life, and leisure, and knowing that it's okay to relax sometimes—and that in fact that it's important for one's mental, physical, and emotional health to do so on a regular basis. Something that Americans emphatically do not do enough!

> "The most important thing I've learned by living in France is taking the time to enjoy life, not identifying myself by what I do, but by who I am. For example, I consider myself a first class flâneuse, and I owe the elaboration of that activity to living in France where enjoying life (and strolls) is not considered 'lazy' and purposeless. In France, unlike in the States, you don't need to be busy **doing** all the time. You can actually sit around and just do your thing. If you look around you in cafés, you'll

> *see that's what a lot of people are doing—chatting, kissing, working, dreaming. I spend a LOT of time in cafés, which I find are the bulwark of French civilization."*

– HARRIET WELTY ROCHEFORT

For the most part this is one of the pleasures—or should be!—for Americans spending time in France, although some Americans don't seem to get it, and instead of enjoying the more leisurely pace of life become frustrated by their inability to do whatever they want to do at whatever time of the day they wish to do it. (Especially whenever they wish to buy things.) One of the things my New York students appreciate less than the leisurely pace of life in Paris is the fact that unlike New York, it is not a 24/7 city. Many shops and even big stores are closed on Sundays, some on Mondays also—though this is beginning to change a bit, and it is a matter of great controversy in France whether this is a good or a bad thing. Stores and other businesses are generally speaking not open as late in the day as they are in the U.S., and many of them are closed for a couple of hours at lunch as well. Restaurants (as opposed to cafés) are closed between lunchtime and dinner. The Metro closes at 1:00 am. And so on.

In a way, the "inconvenience" for shoppers (and diners) at not being able to shop or eat anytime they feel like it, 24 hours a day, 7 days a week is related to the French belief in the importance of taking the time to enjoy life. Because if stores are open 24/7, that means someone has to be there working in the middle of the night, and on Sundays (an important day for relaxing and for families in France), and during lunch, right? And because both quality of life, and *equality of opportunity* for a quality of life are both strong French principles, they think about these kinds of things, and have designed their way of life accordingly.

Another way the importance of taking your time manifests itself in French life is the way that the French can be amazingly patient when waiting in lines. As an American, I am always acutely conscious of the people waiting behind me as I complete a transaction in the post office, grocery story, or wherever. Therefore I always try to quickly move out of the way, or at least to the side, while I put the change in my coin purse, rearrange the contents of my purse or shopping bag, bag my groceries and so on, so that the line can move ahead unimpeded while I finish up whatever I have to do before leaving the place.

French people don't necessarily do this: they take their time with these finishing steps, usually standing in the same place they have been during the transaction: and when they are good and ready, they say a proper "*Merci, madame, et au revoir*" to whoever is serving them. In France there is very little of the huffing and puffing, foot tapping, eye rolling, muttering, and impatient sighing that would go on by those waiting in line if this scene were being played out in the U.S. But there is really no point in complaining about the slower pace of things in France, nor in engaging in the kind of reflexive impatient behavior that is characteristic of Americans. I think a much more productive response is to consider the possibility that we are far too rushed and impatient, and to look at these situations as an opportunity to practice being less so, with grace and good humor.

It is true that sometimes in order to be able to enjoy that leisurely noontime meal, you have to rush to get to the restaurant in time. Or get to the store before it closes for lunch. You cannot just do things whenever you feel like it in France, you have to do things at the time when it is correct to do them. (And when the stores and restaurants are open!)

Some essential services, for example pharmacies, do have 24/7 provisions: most cities have at least one 24/7 pharmacy, and in villages like the one where I live, when there is an emergency that requires the help of the pharmacist, there are ways of reaching them, and they will respond, even after hours.

Americans also often make the mistake of thinking that French waiters are ignoring them when they aren't presented with a bill promptly the way they are in the U.S. These French waiters are not ignoring you: they are allowing you to enjoy your meal quietly and in a leisurely way. They would not think of interrupting you, rushing you, or making you feel pressured to leave before you are ready to do so. (The only time this will happen is if, for example, you are sitting with your morning coffee in the part of the café that they need to prepare for people who will be coming there for their noon meal. Then they will politely ask if they can move you elsewhere, unless you plan to have your meal there too). Sometimes waiters will also need to collect l'addition (the check) before they leave their shift. In that case they will usually apologetically explain that they need to encaisser (cash out). But when they do this, they are not hinting that you should leave: they are just letting you know that it's time for them to leave. You can stay there as long as you want to, as long as the place is open. The only real hint that you should leave a French café is when they start putting the chairs around you upside down on the tables. Then it really is time to leave.

The other misconception somewhat related to this theme is that the French people "don't work." "When do they ever work?" "When do they ever get anything done?" are questions that have been asked by American observers of the French going back at least back to the 18th century, and questions that I myself heard most recently last summer from the students in my CUNY study abroad program.

The French do work, they work a lot. You know they must manage to get *something* done, because they have the world's sixth largest economy. That just doesn't happen without *someone* working *sometime*.

The confusion comes about in understanding the *way* they work. They do not get up in the morning, rush off to work, blast through their day as quickly as they can (eating sandwiches at their desks) in order to "get it over." Then trudge home, exhausted, "grab a bite" for dinner, and maybe answer a few work-related emails, before falling into bed: then wake up the next morning, to repeat the whole dismal grind. (In fact, in 2017 the "right to disconnect" became law, a law that forbids employers in French companies with more than 50 employees to ask their employees to respond to work e-mails during their personal hours. Imagine that!)

Let's take a look at what Edith Wharton observed about French work habits in an essay she wrote in 1917, titled "The New Frenchwoman."

> [The French] conception of "business" may seem a tame one to Americans; but its advantages are worth considering. In the first place, it has the immense superiority of leaving time for living...The average French business man at the end of his life may not have made as much money as the American; but meanwhile he has had, every day, something the American has not had: Time. Time, in the middle of the day, to sit down to an excellent luncheon, to eat it quietly with his family, and to read his paper afterward; time to go off on Sundays and holidays on long pleasant country rambles; time, almost any day to feel fresh and free enough for an evening at the theater, after a dinner as good and leisurely as his luncheon.

Many things have changed in both French and American society since 1917, but I submit that much of what Wharton observed back then has not fundamentally changed at all. Of course, not all Frenchmen make a habit of going to the theater: but I can say, having observed French life in my rural village, that the rhythm of life Wharton described in 1917, with the exception of the mention of the theater, describes perfectly the pace of life I see here. One of the things that has never stopped surprising me is how a people who stay up so late eating their dinner are able to get up so early in the morning, and be more or less chipper. I think it has a lot to do with the more relaxed pace of the lives they live each day. And probably also the knowledge that there will be the heavenly smell of freshly baked bread to greet them when they get up in the morning, and a cup of freshly brewed coffee and a croissant to enjoy in the local café on their way to work.

In other words, something worth getting up for!

I think Americans could do with a little bit more of that kind of approach to life. Don't you?

6

THE IMPORTANCE OF FOOD

When I asked my friend Thierry, the Frenchman who taught my sons French, and who has lived in the U.S. for a long time, what he most admires most about the French, he said, "I admire the epicurean French lifestyle, which stimulates all the senses—food, art, music, and so on..."

Notice what he mentioned first!

So let's talk about food. However, before we do, I have a shocking confession to make. Although I do enjoy good food—very much!—if I answer the question truthfully, I have to admit that I really do fall into the category of someone who "eats to live" rather than "lives to eat."

Please understand: it isn't that I don't like or appreciate good food, I do! It's just that I really don't like having to spend very much time thinking about it, or preparing it. I just like to enjoy it when it's in front of me. I like to enjoy it *thoroughly*. But not think about it too much before or after the fact.

I know. Some of you—especially you "live to eat" types—are probably thinking that living in France is being wasted on me, and I can understand that.

But I assure you, it is not. In my own very simple and uncomplicated way I am most appreciative of the superiority of the food I eat here, even the food I make for myself (and you will probably not be surprised to learn that given the above confession, I am not a great cook.) But my eating habits (and even my cuisine) have improved since I have been spending more time here, simply by the fact that I am immersed in a culture where everything revolves around meals. (It really does!) This makes it harder for me to forget to eat, something I do much more often when I am in the States.

I love being able to get really wonderful prepared food at our local *traiteur*. I love the local, and not-local-but-still-French cheeses I eat here. I love it that fruits each have a unique and distinct taste, and a lovely texture. (They do not all taste more or less the same, and they do not have the consistency of cardboard.) I love the *pâtés* so smooth and rich they are reminiscent of butter. I love the butter! And I love the many unforgettable, and just plain wonderful, French meals I've had, both in restaurants and in the homes of friends.

But because of the above confession, I feel that I am not really qualified to talk very much about food. I will tell you the most important things I know about eating in France, and leave it to the experts—there are so many, and two of them are good friends of mine—to tell you much more.

So here, in a nutshell, is what I know:

1. **In France you have to eat when it is the correct time for eating.** This is linked to the discussion in Chapter 4. What it means is that if you are eating in a café or restaurant, you have to eat your meal at lunchtime or dinnertime, not just anytime you feel like eating. Lunchtime is generally

more or less from noon until 1:30: you should not count on being served lunch if you show up later than that, and in some places 1:30 will be considered too late to start lunch. Dinner never begins before 7 pm, more often around 7:30 or 8:00. You can usually get at least a sandwich in a café at any hour of the day, and maybe if you are lucky an omelet, but you can't order a real meal at any time of day. You just can't. And if you are planning to make your own meal at home, you have to get the ingredients for it before all the shops close for lunch (usually by 12:30, sometimes earlier). Of course many French cities now have "*MacDos*" (McDonald's), and there are other places where you can buy food pretty much all day long. But you don't want to eat in a *MacDos* when you're in France, do you?

2. **When you are eating in a French restaurant (or café, or bistro), you will probably want to at least consider ordering the formule (sometimes called le menu).** The *formule* is not necessarily offered at all times (for example, it usually isn't available on weekends and holidays, and there's often not a *formule* in the evening). But when it is offered, it's the best deal, a far better deal than ordering *a la carte*. The *formule* will most commonly offer you a choice of *entrée, plat*, and *dessert* or *fromage*) (appetizer, entrée, and dessert or cheese). Sometimes you can choose just two of the three for a little bit less. But hey, you're in France! Why not go for the whole thing, and then be prepared to spend *at least two hours* enjoying your meal in a leisurely way. (Remember? We just talked about this in Chapter 5. The importance of taking your time?)

3. **To tip or not to tip, that is the question.** You may have heard that it is not necessary to tip in France, because the tip

is already included in the bill (noted as *service compris*). And this is true. So you don't *have to* tip, and if you don't tip, your French waiter will not be shortchanged and cheated the way waiters who don't receive a tip in the U.S. are. However. I had noticed through the years that many French people (and also long-term Americans in Paris) do tip, certainly not as much as 10 percent, but a little bit. (It is called a *pourboire*.) So I could see that it was a nice and thoughtful thing to do. The question for me was "how much?" So finally I asked David Downie, who has abundant experience eating in restaurants, and who is a thoughtful and generous person, how much one should tip, and his advice was about 3-5 percent. (For small things, for example, for a glass of wine or a cup of coffee in a café, the advice usually is to "just round it up.") So now I do. And you might want to do so also, especially if you are spending a lot of time at your table and/or if you plan to become a "regular." But you don't have to, especially if you don't get good service. (But remember: a waiter leaving you alone is NOT bad service. It's up to you to let him or her know when you're ready to leave.)

4. **Life in France revolves around food.**

    It just does. (And this is, mostly, a good thing!)

Bonus Tip: The French have a great appreciation for the sensitivity and the importance of palate in enjoying a good meal. For this reason, they find the idea (and the practice) of drinking coffee (or milk) with a meal disgusting. (It is definitely not "comme il faut.") Before judging them for this judgment, why not try doing things their way? You might be surprised to find how much more the delicate and complex flavors and textures of food can be enjoyed when you do not coat or otherwise contaminate your palate with such things.

Incidentally, one of the most helpful pieces of advice I have ever received about navigating the everyday challenges of life in France came from a most unlikely source. George Orwell, in his 1933 book *Down and Out In Paris and London*, which is about the working poor, tells the story of his shock at how little he received for the clothing he was forced to sell at a pawn shop when he was down and out in Paris. "When it was too late I learned that it was wise to go to a pawnshop in the afternoon," he wrote. "The clerks are French, and like most French people, are in a bad temper till they have their lunch." Ever since reading those lines I have tried whenever possible to ask for favors, or schedule delicate transactions, in the afternoon, not the morning.

So that is basically all I know. (Well, I know a little bit more than that, but not much.) Also, my friend Ellen said I should add the following important tips, and she is right.

"Never ever call the waiter 'Garçon.' Say monsieur or madame. Don't shout to them from across the room, instead ask for the bill (l'addition) with the universal writing sign. Also, don't just leave the money on the table of a café: make sure the waiter gets it, as theft is common."

- ELLEN HAMPTON

You can find very helpful and comprehensive guidance about French wining and dining from David Downie, author of *A Taste of Paris* and many other books about France and Italy, and in particular about French and Italian cuisine; and also from Gary Lee Kraut, the editor of *France Revisited*, which is a wonderful online publication you should know about anyway. You will learn *so much more* about all the delightful subtleties, nuances, and excellences (and/ or potential pitfalls) of French cuisine from them than you ever could from me.

I think it should also be said that the importance of food is kind of a subset of the importance of *plaisir* (pleasure). And *plaisir* is not just about food—as my boys' French teacher noted in the beginning of this chapter—though the central importance of food in French life cannot be overstated. When I asked my friend Karen Fawcett, who lived for many years in France, what she missed most about France now that she is living back in the U.S., she said, "What do I miss about France? EVERYTHING!! (Well, almost everything.) I miss the architecture every day. I miss the restaurants and lord, do I miss the cafes, and being able to sit and enjoy life and my surroundings the way I don't in the U.S. I miss the gardens, the parks, discovering the unexpected when walking down the street, the wine, the cheese, the wonderful produce, and the FLOWER SHOPS! I miss the small shops, not only for clothing, but specialized ones, such as paper shops. I miss the displays, and the way salespeople so beautifully wrap gifts. I also miss being able to get on a plane in Paris and being in another country within an hour or two...For me, Paris was the center of the world."

Notice that her answer touches not only on *plaisir* and the sensual pleasures of wine, cheese, fresh produce, and so on, but on Tip #4, the importance of being pretty. In fact her answer is a wonderfully comprehensive one, folding in the pleasure in taking one's time as well.

The way salespeople so beautifully wrap gifts, by the way, is one of those small pleasures of life that has to do with the exceptional awareness of and appreciation of visual presentation alluded to in Tip #4. When you are buying a dessert in a *patisserie* or *boulangerie*, or just something in a little shop, you may be asked, "*C'est pour offrir?*" (Is this a gift?) If it is, as Karen has pointed out, they will take great care to wrap it up for you very beautifully indeed. And at no extra charge. (Heavens, they wouldn't think of it! There will be more on why *that* is in Chapter 8.)

7

THE IMPORTANCE OF BEING INTERESTING

Years ago, a friend of mine had a dalliance with a Frenchwoman. When they went their separate ways, neither of them was truly terribly upset—it was a casual affair, and it was over. But she did make certain to tell him before going on her way, that to her, he and his friends were "not interesting." ("I know **many peoples** who are **more interesting** zan you!" were her precise words.)

The importance of being interesting is another thing that Barlow and Nadeau talk about in *The Bonjour Effect*. When I interviewed Julie Barlow for *Bonjour Paris*, and asked her what she thought the hardest thing for North Americans in understanding the French was, she said, "The French think conversation should be interesting, and if that means they run the risk of saying something offensive, they're okay with that. It's better to offend than to be boring! Conversation is like a sport in France."

This explains some of the things that seemed mystical to me when I was first spending time in France. It seemed to me like the French were always wanting to argue about something, even in places like the post office. (Why would you want to have an argument with the clerk in the post office? I just did not get this!) This was very frustrating for me, especially when my ability to argue in French was so much less well developed than it is now. When I would mention this frustration to my French friends they would say, "It's just a game, relax and play it!" But of course it wasn't a very fun game for me. (It's more fun now that I can speak French much better, though I still prefer much less complicated interactions. I guess I have not adopted that French "passion for complication.")

It has been pointed out by a number of commentators that though the French like arguing, they are much less likely to get angry and personally insulted when they do not see eye to eye on some controversial issue. This would explain why they tend to be able to discuss some things (such as politics) more freely than Americans, who are always seeking agreement on controversial issues, and frustrated when they cannot achieve it. Confirming this, one of the French friends I consulted when I was writing this book who has lived for a long time in the U.S. says, "I remember engaging in passionate discussions with friends of drastically different political opinions in a civilized but passionate fashion." But he added, "I also remember kids fighting physically outside the school over their political beliefs."

But that's on the negative side of things. What are the advantages of this focus on being interesting? Well (no surprise here) it seems to me that it tends to develops people who are, on the whole, pretty interesting to be around.

In October of 2010, just a couple of weeks before our midterm elections, and two years into President Obama's first term of office, I drove to Dulles Airport in Virginia to pick up one of our French exchange students. We had not even left the airport parking lot yet when the student, who was 16 years old, said to me, "I just can't wait to ask you two questions, may I ask?" I encouraged him to go ahead, and here were his two burning questions: "Do you think it's true that Obama has failed?" and "What is this 'tea party'?" He then apologized for being "so French," but reiterated that he was really curious about these two things, and eager to hear what I thought about them.

I assured him his questions were good ones, and that I didn't mind at all being asked. And I proceeded to answer them. ("No, I do not think Obama has failed," were my first words.) And in elaborating on that question, and in answering his other one, and the questions that followed, we spent a pleasant hour driving to Silver Spring having a *very interesting* discussion about politics.

I was pretty impressed, though not surprised, that a French 16-year-old would know so much about our election, especially a midterm election, probably much more than most Americans of the same age, and many older ones too. From the time I first spent time in France I had experienced this time and again—Frenchmen and women sometimes knowing more about our politics than I did, certainly knowing much more about our politics than I did about theirs.

This is one aspect of a general characteristic of life in France, in which cultural and intellectual matters are seen as being interesting. It is true that in France you will often hear people say they don't care about (or for) politics. But even those people, generally speaking, have intelligent things to say about the current scene if pressed.

The French verb *ennnuyer* means both "to annoy" and "to be bored." I think this is interesting. It is annoying to the French to be bored! This speaks both to their interest in things that are interesting, and to their generally high opinion of education and intellectual pursuits.

Why is this? I think that at least part of it is a general respect for education, for intellect, and for the importance of learning how to think rationally that is at the foundation of French education.

It's tricky talking about this, because French education is criticized (probably rightfully) for being too authoritative, and too rote, teaching kids to repeat what they have been taught rather than to think for themselves. And yet the result of French education seems to be people who are generally better able to express themselves intelligently, and in fact better able to think rationally, than the American system, which stresses creativity and individuality over rote learning. Perhaps it is because Americans do not receive training in the art of thinking itself—let's call it "philosophy," or "debate," or "rhetoric" for now—that they end up being not very well equipped to express their own opinions in a way that is clear and intellectually sound, and (probably even more importantly) are prone to being unable to see through cant and nonsense in others, or to argue effectively against it. One is tempted to conclude that somewhere in the large middle region between the two approaches is some perfect form of education. (The optimism just expressed, by the way, is a typically American point of view. We just keep thinking perfection is attainable, despite all evidence to the contrary! We call this optimism: Europeans call it naiveté.)

Here is an example of what I'm talking about: every year in the late spring, French teenagers, most of them having studied intensely for months, take a very important exam which means the difference between their going on to studies in the university system, or going on to prepare for a trade. (Learning a trade, by the way, is not viewed as "second rate" in France, as it tends to be, at least by many people, in the U.S. Rather, learning how to practice one's métier with excellence, whatever the métier is, is another important value in

French life. Also, before the "university" track and the "trade" track diverge, all French schoolchildren have received a pretty effective basic educational formation that includes respect for thinking, and learning how to argue rationally.)

Anyway, back to the exam, which is called the *bac* (it is short for *bacalaureat*). Toward the end of each school year, the *bac* is a subject of general conversation, and a story that is regularly covered by the French media. A reporter will approach a group of students who have just come outside from having taking the *bac*, and will ask them questions about it: "Which question did you choose? Was it hard? Do you think your answer was well-argued?" and so on.

The philosophy part of the exam, which is required for all students, asks essay questions like "Does having a choice mean we are free?" "Do we always know what we really want?" "Is it our duty to seek out the truth?" or "Is the only purpose of working to be useful?"

In a *France 24* article published in 2011, it was explained that the purpose of teaching philosophy to all French high school students was to produce "enlightened citizens capable of intelligent criticism." As I have noted above, it seems to me that most of the time that is what the French education system produces. So I'm not too sure that a loose comparison with American education, and the often expressed view that the American system is better at teaching independent thinking than the French one, is fair or justified. Perhaps the question should be refined, to ask which system is better at producing independent and *intelligent* thought.

Importantly, in my observations of many French individuals of different ages, and from a variety of walks of life, it also seems to me that the interest in intellectual topics doesn't stop with the end of schooling, and it isn't limited to "intellectual types." In the same *France 24* article, it was explained that the main purpose of French students being required to study philosophy was so that they would develop a "capacity for personal reflection" that would allow them to "approach issues thoughtfully." And if you look at the questions above, you will see that although they are clearly philo-sophical, they also have quite practical implications for how to go about making decisions in one's personal life.

This interest in and appreciation for intellectual life also feeds into popular culture. When I was first spending time in France there was a very popular prime-time television program about books that aired on Friday evenings. It was called *Apostrophes*. *Apostrophes* had a long run, from 1975-1990. Today there is another prime-time book program that is also very popular, called *La Grande Librairie* (The Big Bookstore). Can you imagine a highly popular prime-time televi-sion program in the U.S. having such a name? (Not if it was really about books, you can't.) But in France there is a hunger for and enjoyment of philosophical discussions. Pierre-Henri Tavoillot, a professor of philosophy at the Sorbonne, was quoted in the *France 24* article as saying, "I'm often amazed by the number and quality of philosophical meetings that are organized in even the smallest villages across France." He added that their success was "astonish-ing," and said, "If there is one reason to be optimistic about France, this is it."

It was Descartes, who was of course a Frenchman, who famously said, "I think therefore I am." (*"Je pense donc je suis..."*) And indeed, one of the things I find most admirable about the French is the extent to which thinking, and intellectual discourse—or even just a well-constructed, well-reasoned argument in favor of or against something—is generally considered to be a positive, not a negative thing—and something that really everyone should be able to do to some degree. It is not viewed as something for "eggheads." It is, in a word, considered *interesting*.

This is not so in the U.S. This is not to say that there are not plenty of smart people in the U.S. who enjoy intellectual discourse.

It is to say, however, that in many social situations or environments they learn to hide, dismiss, or otherwise minimize their intellectual side because it's not widely appreciated, and it's not worth the trouble to defend it. Just think about an American presidential election during which one candidate (John Kerry) was widely criticized (including by his own staff) for speaking French at a press conference (in France). Rather than take pride in the fact that for once an American presidential candidate was able to function in another language in a professional way on the world stage, many Americans said they voted for his opponent because they thought it would be more fun to "have a beer" with his opponent than with the French-speaking "elite" who ran against him.

I have a one-word response to this kind of reasoning: **really?!?**

I am not suggesting that everyone in France goes around reading philosophy all the time, or that their choice of presidential candidates is always admirable. But I am saying that I think the French apply a different sort of standard when judging their candidates, and that they have in general more respect for intelligent thinking in the electoral process. Marine Le Pen came perilously close to winning the last presidential election: but her poor performance in a televised debate with Emmanuel Macron, which revealed her as unprepared and not really on top of her facts, and her opponent as just the opposite, did a lot to damage her campaign at the last minute, even among some of her strongest supporters.

> "To say someone is an intellectual in France is usually a compliment, whereas in the U.S. it's an insult. This is one of the grand canyons between French and American culture. Hence terms like egghead, pointy-head, smarty pants, etc. don't exist, although in some circles, calling someone an intellectual can be an insult."

> - ELLEN HAMPTON

I am also saying that you do hear the words *a priori* a LOT in France, both on television and in conversation. So far, every time I really want to know that means, I still have to look it up, and I am no dummy. (Merriam Webster defines it as "relating to or derived by reasoning from self-evident propositions." I just looked it up again!) This says to me that there is something fundamental in the French educational system that is lacking in ours—that is, thinking about thinking!

"My admiration for 'the French' is usually individual—I admire the intellectual capacities and forthrightness of a given French man or woman, for instance. Take the current president, Emmanuel Macron. He epitomizes some of the most impressive, admirable qualities of the nation: broadminded; life-loving and moderately hedonistic; forward-looking, yet with one eye constantly scanning the past, respecting tradition and experience; well-educated and unabashedly intellectual; practical and pragmatic without being dull; stylish, and animated by an understated flair or animal charisma. Yet Macron also epitomizes some of the qualities that I find least admirable about the French as a nation: he is as vertically organized as a chest of drawers, as hierarchical as a pyramid, the product of an 'elite' system that leaves millions gasping by the wayside; and while he is pro-European and open to the world, he is also profoundly nationalistic, convinced that the French way, the French model, the French language, French cooking and eating habits, and everything else French, are superior to those of all other nations. Being patriotic and proud of one's heritage can be positive and life-enhancing, and in his case they are, but in the hands of lesser men and women this world view can degenerate into the kind of aggressive, swaggering arrogance or, worse, the defensive paranoia that make so many French people unpleasant as partners when sharing a city, or a professional or sentimental life."

- DAVID DOWNIE

8

THE (RELATIVE) UNIMPORTANCE OF MONEY

When I asked Thierry, my kids' French teacher, what Americans should know when they go to France, one of the things he said was that "talking about earnings is a taboo in France."

I would add that it's not really just *earnings* that it is taboo to discuss. For one thing, unlike in the U.S. where practically the first question anyone asks you at a cocktail party is "What do you do?" in France this is not a question you should ask. Period. I had previously assumed this was because asking what a person does is not only considered no one else's business, a part of *la vie privé*, but because what someone does often suggests their financial status as well. I asked Ellen Hampton why she thought this was so, and she said, "In the U.S. your personal identity comes from your work, and in France it doesn't. You can ask someone what field they work in, and they will be quite vague, unless it happens to be something you have in common, for example teaching, or banking. Then you could move into the specifics of it. But it is generally considered bad form to talk about yourself, which is really, really hard for Americans!"

Americans, when told about this, are inclined to say, "Well, what do they talk about then?" And the answer is, they talk about things of general interest to everyone. Art. Current events. Movies. Books. Travel.

Through a series of personal experiences I've learned that the subject of money seems to be viewed by most French people as just kind of an unpleasant topic, to be avoided as much as possible. Here's an example: some years ago, toward the end of our one-month stay in Paris, the director of the dorm my students were staying in asked one of my students to ask me to come and see her after class. ("Uh-oh," I thought. "Now who has done what?") I dutifully went off to the meeting, wondering what sort of trouble my students had been causing, and dreading learning about it. When I presented myself at her office I was greeted by Mme. D in a very friendly way: she invited me to sit down, and engaged me in a bit of casual chit-chat. ("How are things going? Are your students enjoying Paris?" and so on.) This was all pleasant enough, but I was confused as to why I had been summoned. Finally Mme. D looked down, as if a bit embarrassed, and then she stammered out a hint as to why I was there. "Well, the thing is," she said, avoiding eye contact, "...as we are nearing the end of the fiscal year, and we need to settle our books..." I looked at her, eyes wide, and said (in a very direct, American way), "Oh my God! Did you not get your money?!") Relieved that I had taken the burden of this distasteful topic from her shoulders, she sighed, as if this were something she really didn't want to have to discuss with this nice professor, this professor of literature, and said, "Well, no, not yet..."

"I am **so sorry**," I said. "I had no idea! I will get in touch with my school right away and see that this is taken care of as quickly as possible." She thanked me, and then deftly brought the conversation back to more pleasant topics before seeing me on my way.

In other words, my students—about 20 of them—had been staying in a French dorm for almost a month, and all that the administration had received thus far by way of payment for the rooms was a deposit. Needless to say, if the situation were reversed, with French students staying in a dorm in the U.S., it would not have been allowed to go on for so long. (I am inclined to say the students would have had to sleep in the streets until the bill was paid. Okay, that is probably exaggerating, but you know what I mean!)

Bonus Tip: *One of the things Americans really don't get about the French is that they don't respond in the same way to "money talking" as people in many other cultures. It is not true that you can just buy a French person's cooperation. In fact, trying to do so may even be counterproductive, because many French people find the exertion of this kind of pressure both obnoxious and insulting to their sense of dignity. In general they prefer to extend favors because they think it is the right thing to do, or because they have respect and/or compassion for the person in need of help, rather than because they are being paid for it.*

This is another one of the major cultural differences between life in the United States and in France. It isn't that money doesn't matter to the French: of course it does. They need enough money to meet their basic needs as much as anyone does, and they enjoy the things extra money can buy too. (Probably even more than we do, because of that love of *plaisir*.)

The main difference is in the way there is a clear limit as to how much money matters to the French, and a sense for balancing the need for money with the need for rest, relaxation, and taking the time to enjoy life that is very different in France than in the United States.

This is another thing that my students always remark on when they arrive in France, and they see businesses closing up during the height of the summer tourist season (or on Sundays; or for a few hours every afternoon). "Don't they realize they are missing out on a lot of business?" they sometimes ask me.

Of course they do, I say. They are not stupid! But they also believe that taking time to enjoy their lives and their families is important too, and that if all you ever do is work, work, work, you're giving up the chance to do that. You can't put off everything you want to do for retirement, as so many Americans have learned the hard way, to their regret.

The main difference, really, is that Americans don't seem to know when to stop. Edith Wharton pointed this out too, in "The New Frenchwoman" essay. "Americans are too prone to consider money-making as interesting in itself," she wrote.

> They regard the fact that a man has made money as something intrinsically meritorious. But money-making is interesting only in proportion as its object is interesting. If a man piles up millions in order to pile them up, having already all he needs to live humanly and decently, his occupation is neither interesting in itself, nor conducive to any sort of real social development in the money-maker or in those about him...To see how different is the French view of the object of money-making one must put one's self in the place of the average French household. For the immense majority of the French it is a far more modest ambition, and consists simply in the effort to earn one's living and put by enough for sickness, old age, and a good start in life for the children.

Of course, it is not only, or always, greed that drives that American grind of work-work-work. It is also that many of the things Wharton mentions as being the essentials in life—"enough for sickness, old age, and a good start in life for the children"—is for the most part taken care of in France by the French government. This is not so in the United States. I am quite sure that the all-too-many Americans who work two and three jobs in order to meet the basic needs of their families would be very happy to not have to do so. The problem is not that all Americans are workaholics. But somehow along the way—even though we are one of the richest countries in the world, operating within a democracy where supposedly "we the people" have the power to impact our lives—we have not managed to form a society where these things are considered basic rights, and we have not been able to agree that as a collective we should be able to arrange for everyone to have them. In this regard we have failed where the French have succeeded: we have failed, in Wharton's words, to find a way to bring about "real social development."

About 10 years ago my husband was injured at our home in France. It was a freak accident in which one of the tendons in his leg was almost completely severed, and which required immediate emergency surgery. Our village is about an hour away from the nearest big city: when the local volunteer ambulance service came to pick him up that is where they took him, and that is where he received surgery later that same night. Though neither the hospital nor the surgeon would have been considered "star quality" (and though probably many Americans would have insisted on being flown home immediately for "proper" medical treatment), the surgery was successful, and my husband's recovery was rapid and complete. There was a great deal of post-operative care provided, including nurses and a doctor who came to our home to check on his progress, and to dress his wounds post-surgery. The cost for all of this was a fraction of what it would have cost in the States, and no one spoke to us about the cost of anything at all until they were preparing him for discharge from the hospital. At that point I was asked to talk to someone in the hospital finance department. She knew we were Americans, and everyone around the world knows about the outrageous state of health care for Americans. So she was almost wincing as she asked me the first question: whether we had insurance. (We did.) Visibly relieved, next she asked me if I knew about how much of the expense we would be responsible for ourselves. (At the time, our American insurance did cover us while we were abroad: today, most American health insurance policies do not.) I told her that I thought we would be responsible for about 20 percent of the total charges. "Well, if you could pay just that part now, and give me the information about your insurance company, we will take care of the rest," she said. The cost was low enough that I was able to put 20 percent of the bill on our credit card, and not worry about it. And, good for their word, the hospital followed up with our insurance company and took care of the rest. Whatever dickering there may have been about the charges or the coverage, we never heard another word about it. Amazing!

The main point of this anecdote is that throughout this experience, the main focus of everyone we dealt with was on the fact that this was a medical emergency, and the most important thing was to save this patient's leg. The implication was that the matter of how to pay for it could be taken care of later—and the accompanying actions supported it.

Isn't this really the way it should be?

"The lessons of the French Revolution are never far from the surface in France. Unlike in America, where wanting to be rich is considered to be a fine, even a laudable concept, that idea is downright appalling to the French. There's a sense there that everyone in the society is in it together. This concept doesn't always prevail, of course. Still, it's a commonly-shared aspiration. A beautiful one, I think."

- PENELOPE ROWLANDS

9

Est-ce que ca vaut la peine?
(Is it worth the trouble?)

Sometimes when I see friends back in the U.S. we get on the topic of this book: that is, the little (but many) things that a person needs to do in order to be treated well and have a good time in France.

Occasionally people tell me that they went to France, and that even though they didn't speak a word of French, they were treated very well and they can't imagine what people are talking about when they say the French are "rude, arrogant, and they hate Americans."

I always have a little bit of trouble believing this, but maybe it's true. (Or maybe these friends are not quite as attuned to what a French insult is like as I am. It is, like the French, often quite subtle, but nonetheless real and present.)

Other times, as recounted by so many American tourists who have returned from France unhappy with the experience, it is not one bit subtle, not at all!

In any case, I think—as I have just spent **this whole book** saying—that although the French are a wonderful people, with many wonderful qualities, flexibility is not one of them. And that learning the rules that govern good behavior according to their definitions, and following them, can go a long way toward improving the experience of being in France.

Sometimes when I start to explain to these friends what I mean by this, and what some of the rules are, they look at me with one of those curious looks. Which I believe in this case means, "Is it really such a great place to go? And you *like* these people? Is it really worth all that trouble?"

Of course my answer to all three of these questions is a clear, unhesitating, complete and total, **Mais OUI!!!**

And, as I've explained earlier, for me it doesn't even seem so much like trouble. To me it is a psychologically fascinating, endlessly challenging, almost always enriching intellectual pursuit that has kept me happily "playing the game" of getting the French to like me, for nearly 40 years.

It's not everyone's cup of tea, I suppose. Those people—especially the ones who really do like tea—might want to go England instead. (Many of them do.)

But, as I used to say to my family, every year, when we returned from one more wonderful summer spent in France, "Wow, that was great!" Then I would add, "I know the world is full of wonderful places to go, and fascinating things to see. But if you ask me where **I** want to go next, my answer is almost always going to be the same: How about next time we go to France?"

10

CHAPEAU!
CREDIT WHERE CREDIT IS DUE

Lest I (and my friends) leave you with the impression that Americans in France are just out to criticize our generous hosts, who are after all sharing their beautiful country with us, here are some of the answers I got when I asked my American friends who have lived in France to answer the question, "What do you like or admire most about the French?"

> "The French value quality of life, and people take the time to appreciate aesthetics. I love many of their values. I admire not having to acquire everything for the sake of keeping up 'with the Joneses.' I admire their wanting to discuss issues rather than just day-to day happenings. I like their emphasis on family, their love of the arts, and the fact that they travel..."

- KAREN FAWCETT

"I admire their style, their love of aesthetics, their ability to take pleasure in the small and exquisite. I have a chapter in my book "Joie de Vivre" titled "Small is Good." It's my favorite chapter."

- HARRIET WELTY ROCHEFORT

"I like the French sense of morality most of all. I admire that they invented the concept of pacifism, and that they don't believe in capital punishment (after their grand history of such a barbaric idea). And I love that they truly believe everyone is entitled to be treated fairly."

- ADRIAN LEEDS

"I like the way the French treat people as a community with social needs, offer public spaces to hang out in, public transport to get to and fro, public hospitals for treatment, public schools for education. The infrastructure is excellent, and yes, we pay taxes to fund it, but it is absolutely worth it. I am continually shocked by the way American communities rely on private corporations to provide the public sphere. It's not their job, and they do it badly. I love France, and getting to spend most of my adult life here has been a privilege. It has offered an intellectual whetstone and moral compass, as well as an overflowing fountain of art, literature, and history to discover on any given day. I didn't know it when I moved here, but it has been a perfect fit."

- ELLEN HAMPTON

"I love how generations are routinely brought together, and how young people communicate so easily and often with their elders... Language is a huge, seductive part of French culture. I love the almost competitive attitude the French have about speaking their language well. Even adolescents there aim to be articulate! For an American, that's wonderfully refreshing."

- PENELOPE ROWLANDS

"While things are far from perfect in France many things work amazingly well: the healthcare system, public transport, retirement benefits (they are stingy but the checks do arrive), public education from kindergarten through graduate school, public roads and highways, parks and forestlands, and much more....The food and wine are still pretty good, and sometimes excellent or outstanding, despite the alarming numbers of lousy tourist restaurants and cafés serving reheated prefab meals. There is much to be thankful for in this complex old country. So while I see countless French compatriots grousing and grumbling and complaining about almost everything, I rejoice in the knowledge that by and large things here are better than they are in most other places."

- DAVID DOWNIE

GLOSSARY

Adieu/Au revoir These are both ways of saying goodbye, but they convey a very different sense of nuance. *Au revoir* means "until (we) see each other again," so it is actually a very comforting, positive, and optimistic way of parting. *Adieu* means (literally) "to God." If someone says *Adieu* to you, you might ask yourself how you have offended them, and if you will ever see them again: because *Adieu* implies finality.

Bah! This is one of those quintessentially French interjections that is often accompanied by a shrug. (In this case, often a subtle, one-shouldered shrug as opposed to the more exaggerated, two-shouldered shrug that accompanies *bfff*.) Anglophones would spell this phonetically as "bah," but the French spell it phonetically "ben," which you often see in cartoons. It is a milder form of disdain than that expressed by *bfff*, and sometimes is not disdainful at all, but is merely a verbal filler (like "um" or "ah" or "well..."), and often followed by *alors*. Occasionally you will hear all three of these together: ("Bff, bah, alors...")

Bfff! (Or **pfff!**) (Not to be confused with *boeuf*.) As explained in the discussion of *bah*, this is a way of expressing disdain or dismissal.

In September 2017, Roger Cohen wrote a wonderful and very helpful essay about the rich and complex meaning of this expression in the *New York Times*. (Bof is how he spelled it, but with all due respect to Mr. Cohen, I think my spelling is much closer to the way it sounds.) In any case, his essay is well worth reading.

Bien *élevé*. This means (basically) to be polite, to have good manners. But its literal meaning is well-bred or well-raised (the verb *élever* means "to be raised"), and it is very important to be well-bred in France. It is a huge insult to be called (or simply considered) *mal élevé*. Unfortunately, many normal American habits would mark many of us as being *mal élevé*, according to the rules of proper French behavior. Whether you knew it or not when you bought this book, that is one of the reasons you bought it: to know how not to seem *mal élevé* to the French. See (especially) Tip #1.

Bise This is the famous double-cheeked (or sometimes triple, or even quadruple-cheeked) French kiss of greeting (and often of departure as well). Which side you start on, how many kisses, whether you make a smooching sound or not, and who you should *bise* and who you should just shake hands with is a source of eternal mystery to Anglo-Saxons, and some French people say it's not always all that clear to them either. *Bisous*, which is a term used more often in writing, is warmer and more familiar than *bises*. It means "little kisses" and the sense of it feels closer to our writing "hugs." But French people do not hug, not very much. They *faire la bise*. French children are taught to *faire la bise* from a very early age. The number of people you are expected to *faire la bise* with in the course of a social event can be quite astonishing to non-French people. However. It should be said that it is a very warm and friendly way to greet people, something I quite miss when I am back in the U.S., when I have to refrain from kissing all the people I am fond of, and whom I haven't seen in such a long time. (Also. It is actually less "germy" than shaking hands. Think about it: it is! It is an **AIR** kiss.)

Bonjour. THE MOST IMPORTANT WORD in the French language. (See Tip #1. AGAIN!)

Bordel The literal meaning is "brothel," but this term is frequently used by nearly all French adults, to mean "a mess." French president Emmanuel Macron caused a HUGE (and to me somewhat astonishing) outcry when, in October 2017, he used the phrase *foutre le bordel*. (He said that employees of a certain company preferred to "*foutre le bordel*"—loosely translated as "mess things up"—rather than to look for work). But the word *foutre* is, as the dictionary would have it, *très familier*, even crude. (Okay, to be clear, it is the French "F" word.) In a fairly unsuccessful effort to calm the controversy, Macron apologized for his choice of words, though not for the content of what he had said. See also *foutre* (but DO NOT USE this word if you are not French).

Ca se fait pas. "It isn't done." This is the opposite of *comme il faut*. You will most commonly hear this spoken in a stern voice to children. If someone says it to you, you've really stepped over some kind of line, or made a terrible *faux pas*. Good luck figuring out which one!

Caen, Cannes. These are two cities in France. Caen is in Normandy, and was the scene of intense fighting during the liberation of France in 1944. It is pronounced very much like the word *quand*. Cannes is the town in the South of France where the famous film festival takes place. The "a" in Cannes is a "short a," and because there are two "n"s, the "n" is heard much more clearly in Cannes than in Caen. The best way to hear the difference is to head to the Internet for some of those wonderful (free) pronunciation guides. Listen, listen, listen again, and then keep trying it yourself until you get it right!

C'est dommage/Tant pis Both of these phrases translate as "too bad," but the tone and implication is totally different. *C'est dommage* is the phrase you use to express sincere sympathy for a bad situation. *Tant pis* is not sympathetic at all: it is almost like saying "Well, tough shit..."

C'est impossible. C'est pas possible. C'est pas evident. The first two phrases mean, "It's impossible." (But don't worry: it's definitely not. See Chapter 2 to find out how to make it possible.) The third one means, "It's not gonna be easy..." And that is probably true.

C'est pas de ma faute means "It's not my fault..." You know how the British are always competing with other to claim responsibility for accidental errors? ("Sorry, my fault." "Oh no, really, it's my fault..." and so on...) Well, the French tend to *never* admit fault. This may well be because they are raised in a culture that is so focused on being *correct* and doing things *comme il faut*, and they are used to being called *nul* ("a nothing") when they fail to be perfect. (!) That kind of treatment could make one a bit defensive, no? So my feeling about this is, why not just give them a break. It's hard enough trying to be perfect all the time.

Comme il faut. "The way it must be done." (See also, *correct*.)

Correct. Being *correct* is very important in France. Being *correct* means doing things *comme il faut* (the way they must be done). The French always know how do things *comme il faut*, and just in case you are wondering, when there is more than one way to do something, it is the French way that is the right, and *correct*, way. **Always.** If you are American, this should not really bother you, since Americans generally speaking do not care at all about doing things *comme il faut*. In fact, we are famous among the French for doing *n'importe quoi* (any old thing). Our casual, unpredictable habits are shocking (or at least astonishing) to them. But we really don't mean to be rude: we can't help it, that's just the way we are.

Débrouillard, débrouillarde, se débrouiller. A *débrouillard* (male), or *débrouillarde* (female) is a person who knows how to *se débrouiller*, which can be loosely translated as to "manage" or "get along." But the meaning of this verb is much stronger than these translations suggest. What it really means is to manage NO MATTER WHAT. It means to surmount WHATEVER OBSTACLES (often, but not always, bureaucratic ones) one may encounter in order to do what one has to do. It also implies a certain amount of cunning, strategic thinking, or what have you. To be called a *débrouillard*, make no mistake, is a compliment. If you ever choose to move to France you will probably need to be a *débrouillard* just to get through all the red tape involved in securing your visa. (See also *Système D*.)

Du coup is a verbal "filler," and you will hear it a lot in France. It is basically equivalent to our "And so..." It doesn't mean much of anything. Coup on the other hand, can mean a lot of different and useful things, for example un *coup de téléphone* (a telephone call), un *coup de main* (lend a hand), *boire un coup* (to have a drink), and of course *coup d'état*.

Embêter, emmerder, ennuyer, agacer. All of these verbs mean roughly the same thing: to annoy. The literal translation of the first one is "to make stupid." The second means to "put in shit." The third means both to bore and to annoy, and I think it is very interesting that the two things are more or less equivalent in France. The French do like things to be interesting! (There's more on this in Chapter 7.) The final one, which you will hear the least often, is the most polite way of saying it. You will most often hear this word used by people "of a certain age" who are also quite well bred (*bien élevé*).

Flâner. See Chapter 5 for a discussion of this word, which means basically—in Harriet Welty Rochefort's words—to "hang out without feeling guilty."

Flute! This is a very polite way of expressing dismay, more or less equivalent to "Darn!" or "Gosh!" or maybe "Oh, fudge!" (Does anyone say that anymore?) A *flute* is also a special kind of wine glass used to serve champagne. As far as I know, the two meanings have nothing at all to do with each other.

Foutre This is a VERY CRUDE word that it's best for nonnative speakers not to use. But you will hear it. A lot! *Je m'en fous* means basically "I don't care," but it is closer to saying "I don't give a f**k." This is the verb that got Emmanuel Macron into hot water early in his first year of office as president (*foutre le bordel* is the exact phrase he used, making it doubly crude). In the ensuing flap, although EVERYONE agreed that EVERYONE uses this word all the time, most commentators also said something along the lines that *le président de la République* should not use this phrase in public.

Grève This is the very first new word I learned when I arrived in France for the first time, and I learned it in the first 24 hours. It means "strike," and it is kind of a national pastime. The French strike all the time, except for example, during the summer when they have to take their five-week vacations, and there's no time for it. Unlike the all-too-rare strikes in the U.S. (because the unions have basically all been busted), strikes in France are usually not total work stoppages: they are more like slowdowns designed to annoy everyone, and get everyone's attention, as well as (of course) to gain the workers' demands. When there is a rail strike, for example, the public will be advised as to when there will be strike days; which trains will run and which will be cancelled; and will be offered advice as to how passengers can work around the strike. The strikes are annoying but they are also extremely well organized. Very French!

Grogner/raler/se plaindre These three verbs all mean more or less the same thing: to complain. (*Grogner* is "to growl," *raler* is "to rail or grumble," and "*se plaindre*" means to complain). The French are great complainers, and it is one of the things about them that Americans just don't get. I mean, they have this wonderful country with beauty everywhere you look, some of the best cuisine in the world, an extraordinarily beautiful language surrounding them, social protections from cradle to grave, and all they can do is complain? Another mystifying factor. It may be, as David Downie says, that since they love to complain, maybe it can't really be counted as a sign of unhappiness.

Hôtel in French just means "a big, important building." So, for example, l'Hôtel de Ville is a city hall; and l'Hôtel Biron in the Rodin Museum is just the spacious house in which Rodin and other late-nineteenth-century squatters (squatters like Isadora Duncan, Jean Cocteau, Matisse, and Rilke, among them) lived before it was eventually taken over by Rodin, then given to the French government upon his death, to be made into a museum.

Interdit means "forbidden." (So does **défense de**...) If something is *interdit* or *défendu*, you are not allowed to do it. For example, in many Parisian parks the *pélouse* (which is the lawn, or the grass) is *interdit*. (Or it may be *pas autorisé*). This means you cannot walk (or sit, or lie down) on it. You can only sit (or lie down, or walk) on grass that is *autorisé*. If you are lying, or sitting, or walking across grass and a *gendarme* starts to wave his finger at you, and/or blow a whistle, you are doing something that is *interdit*, and you should stop doing it right away, and indicate somehow that you are sorry (*désolé*), you didn't know...

Joie de vivre. This phrase, which is, after all, French, leads us to an interesting paradox about French life and character. For the French are not really known as much for being full of joie de vivre as they are for being a rather pessimistic people. However, they are also known for their love of plaisir—think "Gay Paree." Therein lies the paradox. (And by the way, the French love paradox, because they love philosophy.)

Laïcité is translated as "secularism." It is a very important concept in French life, and understanding it is important if you want to understand, for example, all the fuss about Muslim women wearing headscarves in France (whether or not they can, or should, and where, and when they are, or are not, allowed to do so, and why it is important). Secularism became a deeply instilled and entrenched concept in the French psyche during the French Revolution, when the aristocracy and the Church were declared the enemies of the people. There are many ironies about how important laïcité is in modern French life and culture: one of them is how many Catholic holidays—not just the major ones but others too, like Pentecost (which is celebrated 50 days after Easter); the Ascension of Christ (10 days before Pentecost); and the Assumption of the Virgin Mary (August 15)—are still national public holidays in France, despite the fact that it is one of the least "practicing" Catholic countries in the world. (Although 88 percent of French people are Catholic, at least culturally, according to a 2010 poll only 27 percent of them believe in God, and my guess is that a large percentage of the believers are probably not Catholic.) Another irony is the strength of feeling the French attach to their belief in secularism: it is almost like a religious fervor about the importance of secularism.

Mal élevé The opposite of bien élevé, that is, "ill mannered." You don't want to be called this. If you read this book carefully and follow at least the five most important tips, you can probably avoid it.

Même pas peur This phrase came into frequency in response to the terrorist attacks in Paris in 2015. Loosely translated it is a defiant expression that means "not even afraid" or "you don't scare me." What it implies is in this context is "We are not going to change our lives for fear of terrorism." So, it is basically the French version of "Keep Calm and Carry On." Bravo for the French!

Merde This word means "shit," and although it is certainly just as vulgar, or perhaps more precisely, just as scatological, as the English word "shit," it is also much more loosely used by the French, or at least it is used casually sometimes in contexts that we would probably would not use it. (At other times, especially when it is combined with other vulgar words, such as *putain* and *bordel*, it is perfectly clear that the intent is to be vulgar, or at least to express extreme vexation.) My own personal opinion about this difference is not that the French are more vulgar than Americans, but that they are both more earthy and less puritanical.

Métier can refer to either a profession or a craft. The French take great pride in their *métiers*. It is one of the best things about France, this pride of craft, and of work. It is one of the reasons everything takes longer in France (another reason is all that time given to eating and relaxing). But the result is, as you've heard and perhaps experienced, an excellence of products and services that the French are right to be very proud of.

Mince! This is another very polite way of expressing dismay (similar to "*Flute!*"). Its literal meaning is "thin." Don't ask me!

Monnaie This means "change" (as in having exact change). *Espèce* means "cash" (as opposed to a check, or a credit card (which is called a *carte bleu*).

Napoleon If the first thing that comes to your mind when you hear the word "Napoleon" is "dictator," you're not alone. (If you think of a pastry, you should know that the name for this dessert pastry in France is *millefeuille*. They will be very confused if you ask for a Napoleon in a pastry shop in France. But I digress...) "Dictator" is the main image that Anglophones have of the diminutive Corsican who became an Emperor of France, and who extended French power well beyond French borders until he met his match, first in Russia, and then (definitively) at Waterloo. But the French have a much more nuanced and complicated understanding of who Napoleon was, and it is important to understand that much of contemporary French society is his legacy. It was Napoleon who, after the chaos of the French Revolution, established the French legal system. He also established the educational system, which—significantly—for the first time provided a pathway for people of modest means to succeed—a meritocracy—as opposed to having to be born into the right class. He also established the French administrative system, which, for all the complaining the French and everyone else do about it is, one has to admit, extremely well organized. And if there is anything the French like, it is order. (See Chapter 4 for more on this.) So, you should understand that although many French people recognize those aspects of Napoleon's character (and reign) that were not at all admirable, to make a blanket negative statement about Napoleon is in a way making a blanket negative statement about France and French society as well. So. You shouldn't diss Napoleon in France.

Plaisir Like *flâner*, this is another one of those words that brings out some of the most profound cultural differences between Latin cultures and Anglo-Saxon ones. *Plaisir* simply means pleasure, which in French culture is a very positive concept: and as we all know, pleasure is often not viewed as positively in Anglo-Saxon cultures. (The French know this about us too, and it is the main reason they so often talk about our *puritanisme*.) The love of and respect for *plaisir* is one of the main reasons underlying many important things about the French and their culture, from their famously long vacations to their famously wonderful *art de vivre*, and their fine cuisine.

Putain This word means, literally, "whore," but in common usage it is more like our word "shit." (That is, it is not polite, but almost everyone says it. A lot.) You will hear this word ALL THE TIME, often in combination with other "bad words" (*putain de bordel de merde* is one such common combo). But YOU probably should not say it, unless you want to be laughed at, or risk saying it at the wrong time, or to the wrong person. (You should also be advised that if you were to pronounce the name of Vladimir Putin the normal way, following the usual rules of French pronunciation, it would sound just exactly like *putain*. That is why they pronounce his name Pou-teen.)

Ras le bol is a way of saying someone "has had it," is "fed up," or is "sick and tired" of something. This concept fits very well with the fondness of the French for complaining. It is kind of a handy shorthand way of saying you're unhappy without having to go into all the details.

Reims Okay, now here maybe someone was being a little bit mean (or just ridiculous), when they came up with the correct pronunciation for this French city, which is the city in which many of the French kings were crowned, in the Cathedral. So, are you ready? The way this word is pronounced is "Rance." (It rhymes with the French word *prince*, or the American way of pronouncing "France.") The English pronounce it just the way it looks (Reems) which is one more reason why the French and the British are probably *never* going to get along.

République Since 1792, the French form of government has been a series of republics, interspersed with empires and monarchies, and one very brief period of a communist government, under the Paris Commune, in 1871. They are currently in the Fifth Republic. The American system of government is also a republic. Unlike Americans, most French people know what is meant by a republic, and the sanctity of their republic is very important to them. I never really understood how deep this sentiment was until President Francois Hollande addressed the nation after the terrorist attacks in Paris on November 13, 2015. *"Notre république a été grievement attaqué,"* he said. ("Our republic has been grievously attacked.") I was struck by his choice of words, because in like circumstances Americans do not refer to their form of government, but to their country. I think this suggests that nationalism may be more important in the U.S. than in France: or at least you could say that a deep and abiding (and informed!) belief in their form of government is more important to the French than it is, generally speaking, to Americans. Another way this shows is in the way the French almost always refer to their president as *le président de la République,* whereas Americans refer to the President of the United States.

Soldes. This word means "sales," and you will see it plastered across store windows for several weeks in January-February, and again in late June-early August. These are the two times of year when businesses in France are allowed to conduct sales. Like so many other things in France, there are government rules concerning sales: when they can be held, how much the merchandise can be discounted, the timing of deeper discounts, and so on. There is some regional variation in the exact dates of the sales, but they are always strictly regulated.

Système D is short for *"Système débrouillard."* The *Système* D is a very French concept that means, basically, beating the system (by being a *débrouillard* or *débrouillarde.*) In a society as inflexible and rule-bound as France, it is not surprising that people take delight in finding ways to beat the system. (See also *débrouillard*.)

Terroir The French Embassy in Washington D.C. used to have a full page devoted to explaining the meaning of this very important, and very rich in meaning, French word, and I wish they still did. Basically *terroir* (NOT to be confused with *terreur*, which means "terror") refers to the earth, the soil. But it also refers to everything that the soil of a particular region imparts to the agricultural products of that region, and even to the people. In *Paris France* Gertrude Stein, in remembering her first reaction to Jean-Francois Millet's painting, "Man with a Hoe" says, "The Man with the Hoe made it... ground not country, and France has been that to me ever since, France is made of ground, of earth." France is made "of ground, of earth" to the French too.

Sources Cited

Barlow, Julie and Jean-Benoît Nadeau. *The Bonjour Effect: The Secret Codes of French Conversation Revealed.* London: Duckworth Overlook, 2016.

Downie, David. *Paris Paris: Journey into the City of Light.* New York: Broadway Books, 2011.

Hulstrand, Janet. "The Bonjour Effect: An Interview with Authors Julie Barlow and Jean-Benoît Nadeau." *Bonjour Paris.* September 5, 2017.

Hulstrand, Janet. "Starting a Business in France: Interview with Craig Carlson, Founder of Breakfast in America Diners." *Bonjour Paris.* October 13, 2017.

LeRoux, Gaelle. "Are French students taught to be more philosophical?" *France 24.* June 16, 2011.

Orwell, George. *Down and Out in Paris and London.* New York: Harcourt Brace & Company, 1961. (Originally published by Victor Gollancz Ltd. in 1933.)

Platt, Polly. *French or Foe? Getting the Most out of Visiting, Living, and Working in France.* London: Culture Crossing, 1994.

Stein, Gertrude. *Paris France*. New York: Liveright Publishing, 1970. (Originally published in 1940).

Wharton, Edith. "French Ways and Their Meaning," first published in *The Ladies' Home Journal*, April 1917, 34:12. Reprinted in *Edith Wharton Abroad: Selected Travel Writings, 1888-1920*. Editor, Sarah Bird Wright. New York: St. Martin's Griffin, 1996.

Wiggins, Grant. "Questions from the French Bac in Philosophy." **https://grantwiggins.wordpress.com/2012/09/26/questions-from-the-french-bac-in-philosophy/**

ADDITIONAL RECOMMENDED READING

Alexander, William. *Flirting with French: How a Language Charmed Me, Seduced Me, and Nearly Broke My Heart*. New York: Algonquin Books, 2014.

Barlow, Julie and Jean-Benoît Nadeau. *Sixty Million Frenchmen Can't Be Wrong*. Naperville, IL: Sourcebooks, Inc., 2003.

Carlson, Craig. *Pancakes in Paris: Living the American Dream in France*. Naperville, IL: Sourcebooks, Inc., 2016.

Druckerman, Pamela. *Bringing Up Bébé: One American Mother Discovers the Wisdom of French Parenting*. New York: Penguin Books, 2014.

Greenside, Mark. *I'll Never Be French (no matter what I do): Living in a Small Village in Brittany*. New York: Free Press, 2008.

Rochefort, Harriet Welty. *French Toast: An American in Paris Celebrates the Maddening Mysteries of the French*. New York: St. Martin's Griffin, 2010; *French Fried: The Culinary Capers of an American in Paris*. New York: Thomas Dunne Books, 2001; and *Joie de Vivre: Secrets of Wining, Dining, and Romancing Like the French*. New York: Thomas Dunne Books, 2012.

Taylor, Sally Adamson. *Culture Shock: France: A Survival Guide to Customs and Etiquette*. New York: Cavendish Square Publishing, 2008.

About The Contributors

David Downie was born and grew up in San Francisco, was educated at UC Berkeley and on the East Coast, and has lived in Paris since the mid-1980s. He is the author of hundreds of articles and 16 books, including the award-winning *A Taste of Paris: A History of the Parisian Love Affair with Food*, and other books connected to life in France and Italy. He and his wife Alison Harris, a professional photographer, give customized tours of Paris, Burgundy, Rome, and Liguria (the Italian Riviera). His book *Paris Paris: Journey into the City of Light* is the book I always recommend when someone asks, "If I take just one book with me to Paris, what should it be?"

Karen Fawcett, a journalist (among other things) was the President of Paris New Media, and a founder of Bonjour Paris.com. She was born and raised in Washington D.C. and lived in both in Paris and Provence for more than 25 years. She is now back in Washington, where she enjoys being close to her son and his family. But she comes to Paris at least once a year and travels as much as she can.

Ellen Hampton is a writer and historian from Florida. She worked as a journalist in Latin America, where she met her French husband; they moved to Paris and raised two children. After earning a PhD in history at the *Ecole des Hautes Etudes en Sciences Sociales*, she taught at *Sciences Po* University, and served as resident director for the City University of New York's Paris exchange program. She is the author of the nonfiction *Women of Valor: The Rochambelles on the WWII Front*, as well as *A Playground for Misunderstanding*, a murder mystery that offers insight into Franco/American cultural differences. Her latest project is a novel of historical fiction set in the 11th century.

Gary Lee Kraut, a long-term resident of Paris, grew up in New Jersey. He is the creator and editor of the award-winning online travel magazine, *France Revisited*, and the author of five travel guides to France as well as numerous articles, essays, short stories, and op-ed pieces concerning travel, culture, cross-culture, and expatriate life. In 2012 he was the first foreign journalist to be elected to the board of the *Association des Journalistes du Patrimoine* (France's Heritage Journalists Association), and he was awarded the North American Travel Journalists Association's Gold Prize Award for best Culinary Travel article written for the Internet in 2013. He lectures frequently in the United States and in France, and his customized tours of Paris and other parts of France, especially Normandy and Champagne, offer a unique opportunity for tourists to experience "travel therapy" by engaging in meaningful travel that combines the pursuit of personal interests and passions with destination.

Adrian Leeds was born and raised in New Orleans, and lived in several other U.S. cities before she moved to Paris in 1994. By virtue of raising her daughter in Paris, and through her work helping Americans live and invest in France, she has become deeply integrated into life in France both personally and professionally. Since 1998 she has written several online newsletters a week, in which she shares her life and perspective on things both American and French. Her monthly Après-Midi gatherings in the Marais district of Paris offer Anglophones of any nationality the opportunity to meet others, and to learn from guest speakers on a wide variety of topics. Adrian is also a popular featured real estate agent on the HGTV "House Hunters International" series. She is currently working on a memoir about her exciting adventures—and misadventures—as an American living and working in France.

Harriet Welty Rochefort is not just American: she was born and raised in Iowa. She came to Paris as a young woman, met and fell in love with her French husband, and has lived there ever since. As a freelance journalist, she has written scores of articles on French business, culture, and lifestyle for leading magazines and newspapers, including the *International Herald Tribune*, *The Atlanta Journal and Constitution*, the *Huffington Post*, and *Time* magazine, where she worked as a reporter in the Paris bureau for more than ten years. She also taught journalism in the international program of the *Ecole de Journalisme of the Institut d'Etudes Politiques de Paris* (Sciences Po) in Paris. She is the author of three books—*French Toast*, *French Fried*, and *Joie de Vivre*—each of which explores a different aspect of Franco-American cultural differences. She recently completed her first novel, which is set in France during World War II.

Penelope Rowlands was born in London, and raised there and in New York City. She has lived in France over several long periods, which inspired her 2011 anthology, *Paris Was Ours*. Her books include *A Dash of Daring: Carmel Snow and Her Life in Fashion, Art and Letters*, a biography of the legendary Irish-born editor of *Harper's Bazaar* from 1932-1958. Although she now lives in Princeton, New Jersey, she still spends time in Paris. She is currently working on another biographical project.

ABOUT THE AUTHOR

Janet Hulstrand was born and raised in Minnesota, and lived for many years in New York City and Washington D.C. She first went to France at the age of 25, and since then has spent as much time there as she can. She currently divides her time between Essoyes, a village in southern Champagne, and various parts of the United States. She writes frequently for *Bonjour Paris, France Today, France Revisited,* and for her blog *Writing from the Heart, Reading for the Road.* Since 1997 she has taught "Paris: A Literary Adventure," a class she created for the City University of New York, every summer in Paris. She also teaches classes at Politics and Prose bookstore in Washington D.C.; and leads book groups at the American Library in Paris, and "Writing from the Heart" workshops in Essoyes. She is the coauthor of *Moving On: A Practical Guide to Downsizing the Family Home* and the blog *Downsizing the Home: Lessons Learned.* She is currently working on a literary memoir, *A Long Way from Iowa.*

—